50 *Fabulous* Knit Aran Stitches

by Rita Weiss

Leisure Arts, Inc.
Little Rock, Arkansas

Produced by

Production Team

Creative Directors: Jean Leinhauser and Rita Weiss

Technical Editor: Ellen W. Liberles

Photographer: Carol Wilson Mansfield

Pattern Tester: Kimberly Britt

Book Design: Linda Causee

Published by Leisure Arts

© 2009 by Leisure Arts, Inc.,
5701 Ranch Drive
Little Rock, AR 72223
www.leisurearts.com

Although we have made every effort to be sure that these instructions are accurate and complete, we are not responsible for any typographical errors, or mistakes, or for variations in the work of individuals.

Introduction

As an ardent collector of knit patterns, I have always been fascinated with the beautiful Aran sweaters that supposedly came from the Aran Islands off the coast of Ireland. I loved the stories that accompanied the patterns.

Not only did each stitch have a special meaning but because the sweaters were supposedly worn by the local fishermen, each family's sweaters were knit with unique designs so that if the fisherman drowned, his body might be identified when it washed up on shore. I loved the thought that cables like those on page 22 and 48 represented the fishermen's ropes while Basket Weave (page 8) symbolized the fisherman's basket filled with his plentiful catch. The Bible was expressed in the Trinity stitch (page 24) and Tree of Life (page 9) which symbolized the path to salvation. Diamonds like those on pages 42 and 64 were the shape of the fishing net so they indicated success.

A lovely story, but unfortunately today's historians tell us that it is all a myth !! It's not true.

Aran knitting as we know it was probably invented in the early part of the last century by some local women who saw it not only as a way to make sweaters for their families but as a source of income. In the 1930s a man living in Germany, who probably had never been to Aran, published an article about the sweaters giving names to many of the stitches, and the magic began. Later other writers embellished the list of meanings for stitches. The meaning of the stitches helped to increase the interest in the sweaters and proved a great marketing tool.

As for the poor drowned fisherman whose family recognized him from the stitches on his sweater, unfortunately that too is fantasy. There is really no evidence that it ever happened. The idea may actually have come from the 1904 play, "Riders to the Sea" by J.M. Synge. In this play, however, there is nothing about particular patterns, and the knitted garment is not a sweater but a sock described by the actress as "it's the second one of the third pair I knitted, and I put up three score stitches, and I dropped four of them."

Imagine how disappointed I was when I discovered the truth! It hasn't, however, stopped me from loving the stitches and from collecting them wherever I find them. Now I love being able to share many of my favorites with you. Naming the stitches hasn't been easy; sometimes I have given you the name of the stitch as it has appeared in many old collections, but sometimes I gave the stitch my favorite name. Aran sweaters were traditionally made in the colors of the earth: browns, beiges, greys. These are the colors that we have used for our stitches.

You won't find any reference to gauge in this book because you can actually work these stitches with any type of yarn you choose not just the Aran yarn used by the island ladies.

What you will find are the words "Panel" and "Multiple". Many Aran sweaters were made in panels employing several panels in the same project. Sometimes the same panel can be repeated or different panels used. Usually the panels were joined by plainer stitches such as Scattered Oats on page 52.

A "multiple" is the number of stitches needed to work one complete unit of the pattern. If the pattern says "Multiple: 8 + 4", you will need to cast on any number of stitches which can be evenly divided by 8: 16, 24, 32 or 40 for example. To this you need to add the "+4" so you will cast on 4 more stitches to the total, giving, for example, 20, 28, 36 or 44 stitches. It is important to remember that the "+" number is added just once.

Whether or not the myth of the Aran knitter using her stitches to create a magnificent project is true, pick up your knitting needles and create your own unique design. You'll have fun doing it.

Contents

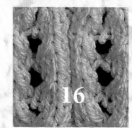

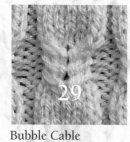

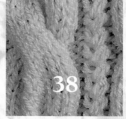

Chain Link Cable

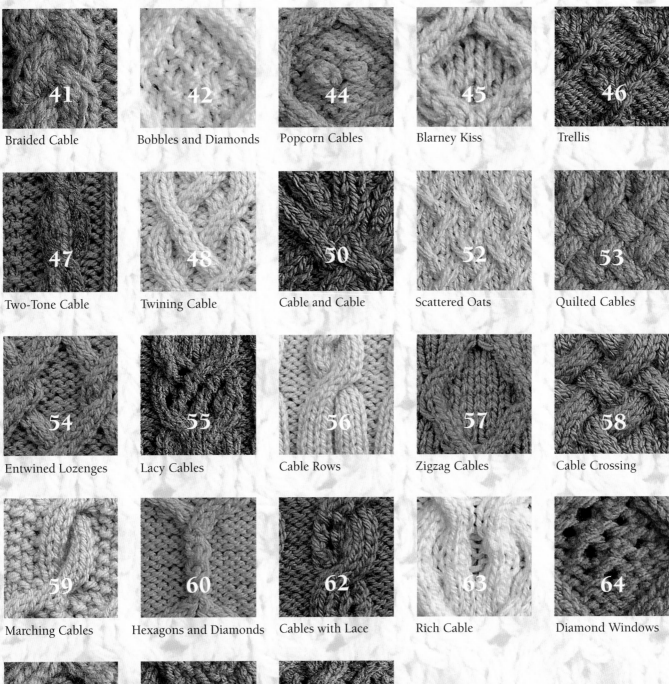

40				
Chain Link Cable				
41 Braided Cable	42 Bobbles and Diamonds	44 Popcorn Cables	45 Blarney Kiss	46 Trellis
47 Two-Tone Cable	48 Twining Cable	50 Cable and Cable	52 Scattered Oats	53 Quilted Cables
54 Entwined Lozenges	55 Lacy Cables	56 Cable Rows	57 Zigzag Cables	58 Cable Crossing
59 Marching Cables	60 Hexagons and Diamonds	62 Cables with Lace	63 Rich Cable	64 Diamond Windows
66 Hourglass Cable	68 Cable Crowns	71 Hearts		

General Directions 73

Cathedral Cables

Multiple: 13 + 2

STITCH GUIDE

T3B (Twist 3 Back): Slip next st to cable needle and hold at back, K2, then P1 from cable needle.

T3F (Twist 3 Front): Slip next 2 sts to cable needle and hold at front, P1, then K2 from cable needle.

SSK (slip, slip, knit): Slip next two sts as if to knit, one at a time to right-hand needle. Insert left needle into fronts of these stitches from left to right. Knit them together.

T5R (Twist 5 Right): Slip next 3 sts to cable needle and hold at back, K2, then work P1, K2 from cable needle.

M5 (Make 5): (K1, YO, K1, YO, K1) in next st.

INSTRUCTIONS

Row 1 (wrong side): Knit.

Row 2: K3; *P3, M5, P1, M5, P3, K4; rep from *, ending last rep with K3 instead of K4.

Row 3: P3; *K3, P5, K1, P5, K3, P4; rep from *, ending last rep with P3 instead of P4.

Row 4: K3; *P3, SSK, K1, K2tog, P1, SSK, K1, K2tog, P3, K4; rep from *, ending last rep with K3 instead of K4.

Row 5: P3; *K3, P3tog, K1, P3tog, K3, P4; rep from *, ending last rep with P3 instead of P4.

Row 6: K3; *P4, M5, P4, K4; rep from *, ending last rep with K3 instead of K4.

Row 7: P3; *K4, P5, K4, P4; rep from *, ending last rep with P3.

Row 8: K1; *T3F, P3, SSK, K1, K2tog, P3, T3B; rep from * to last st, end K1.

Row 9: K2; *P2, K3, P3tog, K3, P2, K2; rep from * across.

Row 10: P2; *T3F, P5, T3B, P2; rep from * across.

Row 11: K3; *P2, K5, P2, K4; rep from *, ending last rep with K3 instead of K4.

Row 12: P3; *T3F, P3, T3B, P4; rep from * ending last rep with P3 instead of P4.

Row 13: K4; *P2, K3, P2, K6; rep from *, ending last rep with K4 instead of K6.

Row 14: P4; *T3F, P1, T3B, P6; rep from *, ending last rep with P4 instead of P6.

Row 15: K5; *P2, K1, P2, K8; rep *, ending last rep with K5 instead of K8.

Row 16: P5; *T5R, P8; rep from *, ending last rep with P5 instead of P8.

Row 17: K5; *P5, K8; rep from *, ending last rep with K5 instead of K8.

Repeat Rows 2 through 17 for pattern.

Basket Weave

Multiple: 20 + 11

STITCH GUIDE

C6F (Cable 6 Front): Slip next 3 sts to cable needle and hold at front, K3, then K3 from cable needle.

C6B (Cable 6 Back): Slip next 3 sts to cable needle and hold at back, K3, then K3 from cable needle.

T4B (Twist 4 Front): Slip next st to cable needle and hold at back, K3, then P1 from cable needle.

T5F (Twist 5 Front): Slip next 3 sts to cable needle and hold at front, P2, then K3 from cable needle.

T5B (Twist 5 Back): Slip next 2 sts to cable needle and hold at back, K3, then P2 from cable needle.

INSTRUCTIONS

Row 1 (right side): P3, K3, *P4, C6F; rep from * to last 5 sts, P5.

Row 2: K5, *P6, K4 ; rep from * to last 6 sts, P3, K3.

Row 3: P3; *T5F, T5B; rep from * to last 8 sts, T5F, P3.

Row 4: K3, P3; *K4, P6; rep from * to last 5 sts, K5.

Row 5: P5, *C6B, P4; rep from * to last 6 sts, K3, P3.

Row 6: Rep Row 4.

Row 7: P3, *T5B, T5F; rep from * to last 8 sts, T5B, P3.

Row 8: Rep Row 2.

Repeat Rows 1 through 8 for pattern.

Tree of Life

Multiple: 9 + 2

STITCH GUIDE

Tbl: Through back lp

BC (Back Cross): Slip next st to cable needle and hold at back, K1tbl, then P1 from cable needle.

FC (Front Cross): Slip next st to cable needle and hold at front, P1, then K1tbl from cable needle.

INSTRUCTIONS

Row 1 (right side): K1; *P3, K3tbl, P3; rep from * to last st, K1.

Row 2: K1; *K3, P3tbl, K3; rep from * to last st, K1.

Row 3: K1; *P2, BC, K1tbl, FC, P2; rep from * to last st, K1.

Row 4: K1; *K2, (P1tbl, K1) twice, P1tbl, K2; rep from * to last st, K1.

Row 5: K1; *P1, BC, P1, K1tbl, P1, FC, P1; rep from * to last st, K1.

Row 6: K1; *K1, P1tbl, K2, P1tbl, K2, P1tbl, K1; rep from * to last st, K1.

Row 7: K1; *BC, P1, K3tbl, P1, FC; rep from * to last st, K1.

Row 8: K1; *P1tbl, K2, P3tbl, K2, P1tbl; rep from * to last st, K1.

Repeat Rows 1 through 8 for pattern.

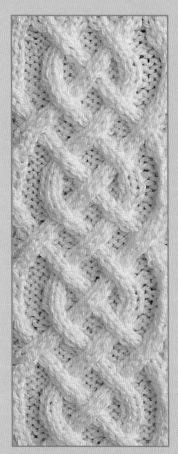

Ropes

Panel: 24 sts

STITCH GUIDE

T3B (Twist 3 Back): Slip next st to cable needle and hold at back, K2, then P1 from cable needle.

T3F (Twist 3 Front): Slip next 2 sts to cable needle and hold at front, P1, then K2 from cable needle.

T4B (Twist 4 Back): Slip next 2 sts to cable needle and hold at back, K2, then P2 from cable needle.

T4F (Twist 4 Front): Slip next 2 sts to cable needle and hold at front, P2, then K2 from cable needle.

C4F (Cable 4 Front): Slip next 2 sts to cable needle and hold at front, K2, then K2 from cable needle.

C4B (Cable 4 Back): Slip next 2 sts to cable needle and hold at back, K2, then K2 from cable needle.

INSTRUCTIONS

Row 1 (right side): P2, C4B, (P4, C4B) twice, P2.

Row 2: K2, (P4, K4) twice, P4, K2.

Row 3: P1, T3B, (T4F, T4B) twice, T3F, P1.

Row 4: K1, P2, K3, P4, K4, P4, K3, P2, K1.

Row 5: T3B, P3, C4F, P4, C4F, P3, T3F.

Row 6: P2, (K4, P4) twice, K4, P2.

Row 7: K2, P3, T3B, T4F, T4B, T3F, P3, K2.

Row 8: (P2, K3) twice, P4, (K3, P2) twice.

Row 9: (K2, P3) twice, C4B, (P3, K2) twice.

Row 10: (P2, K3) twice, P4, (K3, P2) twice.

Row 11: K2, P3, T3F, T4B, T4F, T3B, P3, K2.

Row 12: P2, (K4, P4) twice, K4, P2.

Row 13: T3F, P3, C4F, P4, C4F, P3, T3B.

Row 14: K1, P2, K3, P4, K4, P4, K3, P2, K1.

Row 15: P1, T3F, (T4B, T4F) twice, T3B, P1.

Row 16: K2, (P4, K4) twice, P4, K2.

Repeat Rows 1 through 16 for pattern.

Cable Circles

Panel: 20 sts

STITCH GUIDE

C4F (Cable 4 Front): Slip next 2 sts to cable needle and hold at front, K2, then K2 from cable needle.

T4B (Twist 4 Back): Slip next 2 sts to cable needle and hold at back, K2, then P2 from cable needle.

T4F (Twist 4 Front): Slip next 2 sts to cable needle and hold in front, P2, then K2 from cable needle.

INSTRUCTION

Row 1 (right side): K2, P2, C4F, P4, C4F, P2, K2.

Row 2: (K4, P4) twice, K4.

Row 3: K2, P2, K4, P4, K4, P2, K2.

Row 4: Rep Row 2.

Row 5: K2, P2, C4F, P4, C4F, P2, K2.

Row 6: Rep Row 2.

Row 7: K2, (T4B, T4F) twice, K2.

Row 8: Rep Row 3.

Row 9: K4, P4, C4F, P4, K4.

Row 10: Rep Row 3.

Row 11: Rep Row 2.

Row 12: Rep Row 3.

Row 13: Rep Row 9.

Row 14: Rep Row 3.

Row 15: Rep Row 2.

Row 16: Rep Row 3.

Row 17: Rep Row 9.

Row 18: Rep Row 3.

Row 19: K2, (T4F, T4B) twice, K2.

Row 20: Rep Row 2.

Repeat Rows 1 through 20 for pattern.

Double Cable

Multiple: 20 + 2

STITCH GUIDE

T4L (Twist 4 left): Slip 3 sts to cable needle and hold at front, K1, K3 from cable needle.

T4R (Twist 4 right): Slip next stitch to cable needle and hold at back, K3, K1 from cable needle.

C6F (Cable 6 Front): Slip next 3 sts to cable needle and hold at front, K3, then K3 from cable needle.

C6B (Cable 6 Back): Slip next 3 sts to cable needle and hold at back, K3, then K3 from cable needle.

INSTRUCTIONS

Row 1 (right side): P2; *K1, T4L, (P1, K1) 4 times, T4R, K1, P2; rep from * across.

Row 2: *K2, P5 (P1, K1) 4 times, P5; rep from * to last 2 sts, K2.

Row 3: P2; *K2, T4L, (P1, K1) 3 times, T4R, K2, P2; rep from * across.

Row 4: *K2, P6, (P1, K1) 3 times, P6; rep from * to last 2 sts, K2.

Row 5: P2; *K3, T4L, (P1, K1) twice, T4R, K3, P2; rep from * across.

Row 6: *K2, P7, (P1, K1) twice, P7; rep from * to last 2 sts, K2.

Row 7: P2; *K4, T4L, P1, K1, T4R, K4, P2; rep from * across.

Row 8: *K2, P9, K1, P8; rep from * to last 2 sts, K2.

Row 9: P2; *K5, T4L, T4R, K5, P2; rep from * across.

Row 10: *K2, P18; rep from * to last 2 sts, K2.

Row 11: P2; *C6B, C6F, C6B, P2; rep from * across.

Row 12: Rep Row 10.

Row 13: P2; *K5, T4R, T4L, K5, P2; rep from * across.

Row 14: Rep Row 10.

Row 15: P2; *K4, T4R, K1, P1, T4L, K4, P2; rep from * across.

Row 16: *K2, P8, K1, P9; rep from * to last 2 sts, K2.

Row 17: P2; *K3, T4R, (K1, P1) twice, T4L, K3, P2; rep from * across.

Row 18: *K2, P7, (K1, P1) twice, P7; rep from * to last 2 sts, K2.

Row 19: P2; *K2, T4R, (K1, P1) 3 times, T4L, K2, P2; rep from * across.

Row 20: *K2, P6, (K1, P1) 3 times, P6; rep from * to last 2 sts, K2.

Row 21: P2; *K1, T4R, (K1, P1) 4 times, T4L, K1, P2; rep from * across.

Row 22: *K2, P5, (K1, P1) 4 times, P5; rep from * to last 2 sts, K2.

Repeat Rows 1 through 22 for pattern.

Diamond Boxes

Panel: 24 sts

STITCH GUIDE

Tbl: Through back loop

T3B (Twist 3 Back): Slip next st to cable needle and hold at back, K2tbl, then P1 from cable needle.

T3F (Twist 3 Front): Slip next 2 sts to cable needle and hold at front, P1, then K2tbl from cable needle.

C4FP (Cable 4 Front Purl): Slip next 2 sts to cable needle and hold at front, P2tbl, then P2tbl from cable needle.

INSTRUCTIONS

Row 1 (right side): P4, K4tbl, P8, K4tbl, P4.

Row 2: K4, P4tbl, K8, P4tbl, K4.

Row 3: P3, T3B, T3F, P6, T3B, T3F, P3.

Row 4: K3, P2tbl, K2, P2tbl, K6, P2tbl, K2, P2tbl, K3.

Row 5: P2, T3B, P2, T3F, P4, T3B, P2, T3F, P2.

Row 6: K2, (P2tbl, K4) 3 times, P2tbl, K2.

Row 7: P1, T3B, P4, T3F, P2, T3B, P4, T3F, P1.

Row 8: K1, P2tbl, K6, P2tbl, K2, P2tbl, K6, P2tbl, K1.

Row 9: T3B, P6, T3F, T3B, P6, T3F.

Row 10: P2tbl, K8, C4FP, K8, P2tbl.

Row 11: T3F, P6, T3B, T3F, P6, T3B.

Row 12: K1, P2tbl, K6, P2tbl, K2, P2tbl, K6, P2tbl, K1.

Row 13: P1, T3F, P4, T3B, P2, T3F, P4, T3B, P1.

Row 14: K2, (P2tbl, K4) 3 times, P2tbl, K2.

Row 15: P2, T3F, P2, T3B, P4, T3F, P2, T3B, P2.

Row 16: K3, P2tbl, K2, P2tbl, K6, P2tbl, K2, P2tbl, K3.

Row 17: P3, T3F, T3B, P6, T3F, T3B, P3.

Row 18: K4, C4FP, K8, C4FP, K4.

Repeat Rows 3 through 18 for pattern.

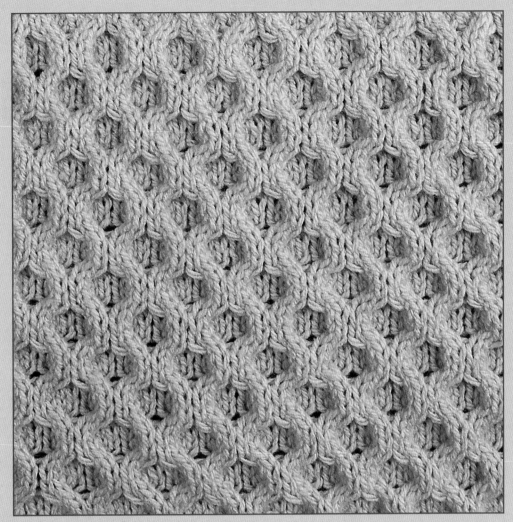

Honeycomb

Multiple: 8 + 4

STITCH GUIDE

C4F (Cable 4 Front): Slip next 2 sts to cable needle and hold at front, K2, then K2 from cable needle.

C4B (Cable 4 Back): Slip next 2 sts to cable needle and hold at back, K2, then K2 from cable needle.

INSTRUCTIONS

Row 1(right side): K2; *C4B, C4F; rep from * to last 2 sts, K2.

Row 2: K2; *Purl to last 2 sts, K2.

Row 3: Knit.

Row 4: K2; *Purl to last 2 sts, K2.

Row 5: K2; *C4F C4B; rep from * to last 2 sts, K2.

Row 6: Rep Row 2.

Row 7: Rep Row 3.

Row 8: Rep Row 4.

Repeat Rows 1 through 8 for pattern, ending with a Row 2 or a Row 6.

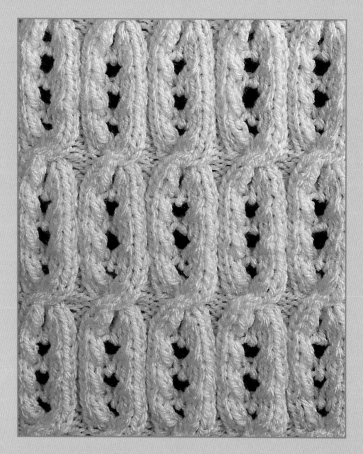

Cable Lace

Multiple: 8 + 2

STITCH GUIDE

Cr6B (Cross 6 Back): Slip 4 sts to cable needle and hold at back, K2, slip 2 sts from cable needle to left knitting needle and K2, then K2 from cable needle.

INSTRUCTIONS

Row 1 (right side): P2, *K6, P2; rep from * across.

Row 2: K2, *P6, K2; rep from * across.

Row 3: P2, *K1, K2tog, (YO) twice, sl 1 as to purl, K1, PSSO, K1, P2; rep from * across.

Row 4: K2; *P2, (K1, P1 into YO), P2, K2; rep from * across.

Row 5: P2, *K6, P2; rep from * across.

Row 6: K2, *P6, K2; rep from * across.

Row 7: P2, *Cr6B, P2; rep from * across.

Row 8: K2, *P6, K2; rep from * across.

Row 9: P2, *K1, K2tog, (YO) twice, sl 1 as to purl, K1, PSSO, K1, P2; rep from * across.

Row 10: K2; *P2, (K1, P1 into YO), P2, K2; rep from * across.

Row 11: P2, *K6, P2; rep from * across.

Row 12: K2, *P6, K2; rep from * across.

Row 13: P2, *K1, K2tog, (YO) twice, sl 1 as to purl, K1, PSSO, K1, P2; rep from * across.

Row 14: K2; *P2, (K1, P1) into YO, P2, K2; rep from * across.

Row 15: P2, *K6, P2; rep from * across.

Row 16: K2, *P6, K2; rep from * across.

Row 17: P2, *K1, K2tog, (YO) twice, sl 1 as to purl, K1, PSSO, K1, P2; rep from * across.

Row 18: K2; *P2, (K1, P1 into YO), P2, K2; rep from * across.

Repeat Rows 1 through 18 for pattern, ending by working a Row 8.

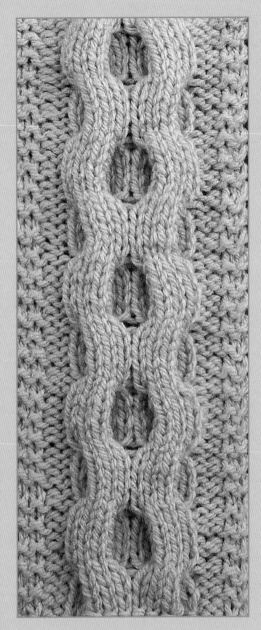

Edged Cable

Panel: 24 sts

STITCH GUIDE

C8F (Cable 8 Front): Slip next 4 sts to cable needle and hold at front, K4, then K4 from cable needle.

C8B (Cable 8 Back): Slip next 4 sts to cable needle and hold at back, K4, then K4 from cable needle.

INSTRUCTIONS

Row 1 (right side): K2, P2, K16, P2, K2.

Row 2 and all even rows: K4, P16, K4.

Row 3: Rep Row 1.

Row 5: K2, P2, C8B, C8F, P2, K2

Row 7: Rep Row 1.

Row 9: Rep Row 1.

Row 11: K2, P2, C8F, C8B, P2, K2.

Row 12: K4, P16, K4.

Repeat Rows 1 through 12 for pattern

Interlocking Cables

Panel: 24 sts

STITCH GUIDE

C6F (Cable 6 Front): Slip next 3 sts to cable needle and hold at front, K3, then K3 from cable needle.

C6B (Cable 6 Back): Slip next 3 sts to cable needle and hold at back, K3, then K3 from cable needle.

Note: *Always slip yarn as if to knit; keep yarn in back of slipped stitch.*

INSTRUCTIONS

Row 1 (right side): K3, P1, sl 1, P1, K12, P1, sl 1, P1, K3.

Row 2: K2, (P1, K1) twice, P12, (K1, P1) twice, K2.

Row 3: Rep Row 1.

Row 4: Rep Row 2.

Row 5: Rep Row 1.

Row 6: Rep Row 2.

Row 7: Rep Row 1.

Row 8: Rep Row 2.

Row 9: K3, P1, sl 1, P1, C6B, C6F, P1, sl 1, P1, K3.

Row 10: K2, (P1, K1) twice, P12, (K1, P1) twice, K2.

Row 11: Rep Row 1.

Row 12: Rep Row 2.

Repeat Rows 1 through 12 for pattern.

Lobster Claw

Multiple: 9

STITCH GUIDE

C3L (Cable 3 Left): Slip next st to cable needle and hold at front, K2, then K1 from cable needle.

C3R (Cable 3 Right): Slip next 2 sts to cable needle and hold at back, K1, then K2 from cable needle.

INSTRUCTIONS

Row 1 (right side): *P1, K7, P1; rep from * across.

Row 2: *K1, P7, K1; rep from * across.

Row 3: *P1, C3R, K1, C3L, P1; rep from * across.

Row 4: *K1, P7, K1; rep from * across.

Repeat Rows 1 through 4 for pattern.

Circled Cables

Panel: 28 sts

STITCH GUIDE

C4F (Cable 4 Front): Slip next 2 sts to cable needle and hold at front, K2, then K2 from cable needle.

C4B (Cable 4 Back): Slip next 2 sts to cable needle and hold at back, K2, then K2 from cable needle.

T4B (Twist 4 Back): Slip next 2 sts to cable needle and hold at back, K2, then P2 from cable needle.

T4F (Twist 4 Front): Slip next 2 sts to cable needle and hold in front, P2, then K2 from cable needle.

INSTRUCTIONS

Row 1 (right side): K2, (K1, P1) 4 times, C4B, C4F, (P1, K1) 4 times, K2.

Row 2: K2, (P1, K1) 4 times, P2, K4, P2, (K1, P1) 4 times, K2.

Row 3: K2, (P1, K1) 3 times, C4B, P4, C4F, (K1, P1) 3 times, K2.

Row 4: K2, (K1, P1) 3 times, P4, K4, P4, (P1, K1) 3 times , K2.

Row 5: K2, (K1, P1) twice, T4B, K2, P4, K2, T4F, (P1, K1) twice, K2.

Row 6: K2, (P1, K1) twice, P3, K1, P2, K4, P2, K1, P3, (K1, P1) twice, K2.

Row 7: K4, T4B, P1, K1, T4F, T4B, P1, K1, T4F, K4.

Row 8: K2, P4, (K1, P1) 3 times, P4, (P1, K1) 3 times, P4, K2.

Row 9: K2, T4B, (K1, P1) 3 times, C4B, (P1, K1)3 times, T4F, K2.

Row 10: K2, P3, (K1, P1) 4 times, P2, (P1, K1)

4 times, P3, K2.

Row 11: K4, (P1, K1) 4 times, K4, (K1, P1) 4 times, K4.

Row 12: K2, P2, (K1, P1) 4 times, P4, (P1, K1) 4 times, P2, K2.

Row 13: K4, (K1, P1) 4 times, C4B, (P1, K1) 4 times, K4.

Row 14: K2, P3, (K1, P1) 4 times, P2, (P1, K1) 4 times, P3, K2.

Row 15: K4, (P1, K1) 4 times, K4, (K1, P1) 4 times, K4

Row 16: K2, P2, (K1, P1) 4 times, P4, (P1, K1) 4 times, P2, K2.

Row 17: K4, (K1, P1) 4 times, C4B, (P1, K1) 4 times, K4.

Row 18: K2, P3,(K1, P1) 4 times, P2, (P1, K1) 4 times, P3, K2.

Row 19: K4, (P1, K1) 4 times, K4, (K1, P1) 4 times, K4.

Row 20: K2, P2, (K1, P1) 4 times, P4, (P1, K1) 4 times, P2, K2.

Row 21: K2, C4F, (K1, P1) 3 times, C4B, (P1, K1) 3 times, C4B, K2.

Row 22: K2, P4, (P1, K1) 3 times, P4, (K1, P1) 3 times, P4, K2.

Row 23: K2, P1, K1, T4F, P1, K1, C4B, C4F, K1, P1, T4B, K1, P1, K2.

Row 24: K2, (K1, P1) twice, P2, K1, P3, K4, (P3, K1) twice, P1, K3.

Row 25: K2, (K1, P1) twice, T4F, K2, P4, K2, T4B, (P1, K1) twice, K2.

Row 26: K2, (P1, K1) 3 times, P4, K4, P4, (K1, P1) 3 times, K2.

Row 27: K2, (P1, K1) 3 times, T4F, P4, T4B, (K1, P1) 3 times, K2.

Row 28: K2, (K1, P1) 4 times, P2, K4, P2, (P1, K1) 4 times, K2.

Row 29: K2, (K1, P1) 4 times, T4F, T4B, (P1, K1) 4 times, K2.

Row 30: K2, (P1, K1) 4 times, P2, K4, P2, (K1, P1) 4 times, K2.

Repeat Rows 3 through 30 for pattern.

Twists and Cables
Panel: 32 sts

STITCH GUIDE

T4B (Twist 4 Back): Slip next 2 sts to cable needle and hold at back, K2, then P2 from cable needle.

T4F (Twist 4 Front): Slip next 2 sts to cable needle and hold in front, P2, then K2 from cable needle.

T3B (Twist 3 Back): Slip next st to cable needle and hold at back, K2, then P1 from cable needle.

T3F (Twist 3 Front): Slip next 2 sts to cable needle and hold at front, P1, then K2 from cable needle.

C4F (Cable 4 Front): Slip next 2 sts to cable needle and hold at front, K2, then K2 from cable needle.

C4B (Cable 4 Back): Slip next 2 sts to cable needle and hold at back, K2, then K2 from cable needle.

T5BR (Twist 5 Back Right): Slip next 3 sts to cable needle and hold at back, K2, then P3 from cable needle.

T5FL (Twist 5 Front Left): Slip next 2 sts to cable needle and hold at front, P3, then K2 from cable needle.

INSTRUCTIONS

Row 1 (right side): P4, K2, P1, K2, P5, K4, P5, K2, P1, K2, P4.

Row 2: K4, P2, K1, P2, K5, P4, K5, P2, K1, P2, K4.

Row 3: P4, K2, P1, K2, P3, T4B, T4F, P3, K2, P1, K2, P4.

Row 4: K4, P2, K1, P2, K3, P2, K4, P2, K3, P2, K1, P2, K4.

Row 5: P3, T3B, P1, T4F, T3B, P4, T3F, T4B, P1, T3F, P3.

Row 6: K3, P2, K4, P4, K6, P4, K4, P2, K3.

Row 7: P2, T3B, P4, C4F, P6, C4F, P4, T3F, P2.

Row 8: K2, P2, K5, P4, K6, P4, K5, P2, K2.

Row 9: P2, K2, P4, T3B, T5FL, T5BR, T3F, P4, K2, P2.

Row 10: K2, (P2, K4) twice, P4, (K4, P2) twice, K2.

Row 11: P2, T3F, P2, T3B, P4, C4B, P4, T3F, P2, T3B, P2.

Row 12: K3, P2, K2, P2, K5, P4, K5, P2, K2, P2, K3.

Row 13: P3, T3F, T3B, P5, K4, P5, T3F, T3B, P3.

Row 14: K4, P4, K6, P4, K6, P4, K4.

Row 15: P4, C4B, (P6, C4B) twice, P4.

Row 16: K4, P4, (K6, P4) twice, K4.

Row 17: P3, T3B, T3F, P5, K4, P5, T3B, T3F, P3.

Row 18: K3, P2, K2, P2, K5, P4, K5, P2, K2, P2, K3

Row 19: P2, T3B, P2, T3F, P4, C4B, P4, T3B, P2, T3F, P2.

Row 20: K2, (P2, K4) twice, P4, (K4, P2) twice, K2.

Row 21: P2, K2, P4, T3F, T5BR, T5FL, T3B, P4, K2, P2.

Row 22: K2, P2, K5, P4, K6, P4, K5, P2, K2.

Row 23: P2, T3F, P4, C4F, P6, C4F, P4, T3B, P2.

Row 24: K3, P2, K4, P4, K6, P4, K4, P2, K3.

Row 25: P3, T3F, P1, T4B, T3F, P4, T3B, T4F, P1, T3B, P3.

Row 26: K4, P2, K1, P2, K3, P2, K4, P2, K3, P2, K1, P2, K4.

Row 27: P4, K2, P1, K2, P3, T4F, T4B, P3, K2, P1, K2, P4.

Row 28: K4, P2, K1, P2, K5, P4, K5, P2, K1, P2, K4.

Row 29: P4, K2, P1, K2, P5, K4, P5, K2, P1, K2, P4.

Row 30: K4, P2, K1, P2, K5, P4, K5, P2, K1, P2, K4.

Repeat Rows 3 through 30 for pattern.

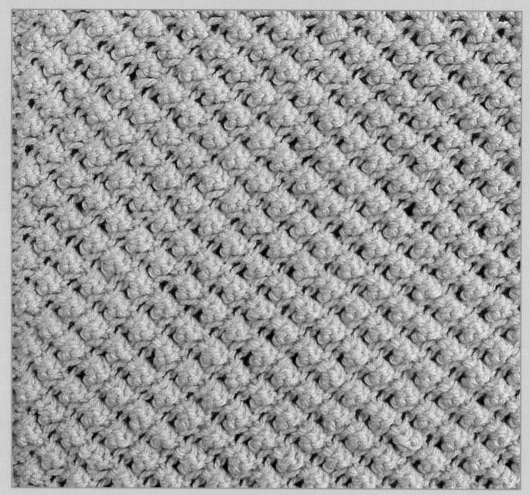

Trinity Stitch

Multiple: 4

STITCH GUIDE

M3 (Make 3 sts): Into next st work (K1, P1, K1).

YF: With yarn in front

YB: With yarn in back

INSTRUCTIONS

Row 1 (wrong side): K2; *M3, YF, P3tog, YB; rep from * to last 2 sts, K2.

Row 2 (right side): K1, purl to last st, K1.

Row 3: K2; *YF, P3tog, YB, M3; rep from * to last 2 sts, K2.

Row 4: K1, purl to last st, K1.

Repeat Rows 1 through 4 for pattern.

Rapunzel's Cable

Panel: 16 sts

STITCH GUIDE

C8B: Slip 4 sts to cable needle and hold at back, K1, P2, K1, then K1, P2, K1 from cable needle.

C8F: Slip 4 sts to cable needle and hold at front, K1, P2, K1, then K1, P2, K1 from cable needle.

INSTRUCTIONS

Row 1 (wrong side): K1; (P2, K2) 3 times; P2, K1.

Row 2: P1; (K2, P2) 3 times; K2, P1.

Row 3: K1; (P2, K2) 3 times; P2, K1.

Row 4: P1; (K2, P2) 3 times; K2, P1.

Row 5: K1; (P2, K2) 3 times; P2, K1.

Row 6: P1; (K2, P2) 3 times; K2, P1.

Row 7: K1; (P2, K2) 3 times; P2, K1.

Row 8: P1; (K2, P2) 3 times; K2, P1.

Row 9: *C8B, C8F.

Row 10: P1; (K2, P2) 3 times; K2, P1.

Repeat Rows 1 through 10 for pattern.

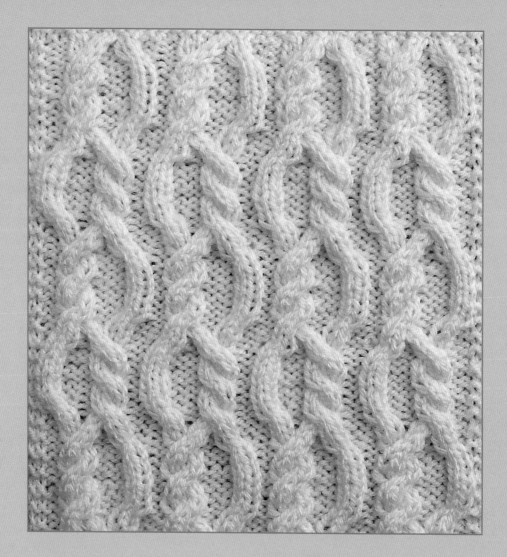

Small Cable

Multiple: 12 + 4

STITCH GUIDE:

C4F (Cable 4 Front): Slip next 2 sts to cable needle and hold at front, K2, then K2 from cable needle.

C4B (Cable 4 Back): Slip next 2 sts to cable needle and hold at back, K2, then K2 from cable needle.

T4B (Twist 4 Back): Slip next 2 sts to cable needle and hold at back, K2, then P2 from cable needle.

T4F (Twist 4 Front): Slip next 2 sts to cable needle and hold in front, P2, then K2 from cable needle.

INSTRUCTIONS

Row 1: K2; *K2, P2, K2, P4, K2; rep from * to last 2 sts, K2.

Row 2 (right side): K2; *P2, C4F, P2, T4F; rep from * to last 2 sts, K2.

Row 3: K2; *P2, K4, P4, K2; rep from * to last 2 sts, K2.

Row 4: K2; *P2, K4, P4, K2; rep from * to last 2 sts, K2.

Row 5: K2; *P2, K4, P4, K2; rep from * to last 2 sts, K2.

Row 6: K2; *P2, C4F, P4, K2; rep from * to last 2 sts, K2.

Row 7: K2; * P2, K4, P4, K2; rep from * to last 2 sts, K2.

Row 8: Rep Row 4.

Row 9: Rep Row 7.

Row 10: K2; *P2, C4F, P2, T4B; rep from * to last 2 sts, K2.

Row 11: K2; *K2, P2, K2, P4, K2; rep from * to last 2 sts, K2.

Row 12: K2; *P2, K2, T4F, K2, P2; rep from * to last 2 sts, K2.

Row 13: K2; *K2, P4, K2, P2, K2; rep from * to last 2 sts, K2.

Row 14: K2; *T4B, P2, C4B, P2; rep from * to last 2 sts, K2.

Row 15: K2; *K2, P4, K4, P2; rep from * to last 2 sts, K2.

Row 16: K2; *K2, P4, K4, P2; rep from * to last 2 sts, K2.

Row 17: Rep Row 15.

Row 18: K2; *K2, P4, C4B, P2; rep from * to last 2 sts, K2.

Row 19: Rep Row 15.

Row 20: Rep Row 16.

Row 21: Rep Row 15.

Row 22: K2; *T4F, P2, C4B, P2; rep from * to last 2 sts, K2.

Row 23: K2; *K2, P4, K2, P2, K2; rep from * to last 2 sts, K2.

Row 24: K2; *P2, K2, T4B, K2, P2; rep from * to last 2 sts, K2.

Repeat Row 1 through 24 for pattern.

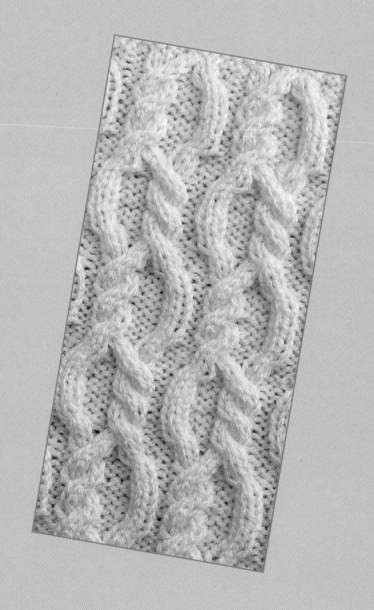

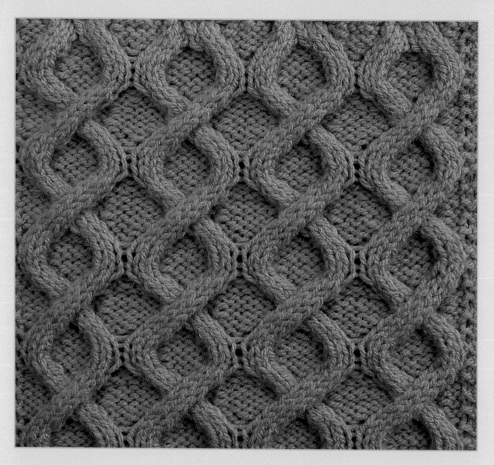

Open Cables

Multiple: 14 + 4

STITCH GUIDE

C6B (Cable 6 Back): Slip next 3 sts to cable needle and hold at back, K3, then K3 from cable needle.

T5F (Twist 5 Front): Slip next 3 sts to cable needle and hold at front, P2, then K3 from cable needle.

T5B (Twist 5 Back): Slip next 2 sts to cable needle and hold at back, K3, then P2 from cable needle.

INSTRUCTIONS

Row 1 (right side): K2; *P4, C6B, P4; rep from * to last 2 sts, K2.

Row 2: K2; *K4, P6, K4; rep from * to last 2 sts, K2.

Row 3: K2; *P2, T5B, T5F, P2; rep from * to last 2 sts, K2.

Row 4: K2; *K2, P3, K4, P3, K2; rep from * to last 2 sts, K2.

Row 5: K2; *T5B, P4, T5F; rep from * to last 2 sts, K2.

Row 6: K2; *P3, K8, P3; rep from * to last 2 sts, K2.

Row 7: K2; *K3, P8, K3; rep from * to last 2 sts, K2.

Row 8: K2; *P3, K8, P3; rep from * to last 2 sts, K2.

Row 9: K2; *T5F, P4, T5B; rep from * to last 2 sts, K2.

Row 10: K2; *K2, P3, K4, P3, K2; rep from * to last 2 sts, K2.

Row 11: K2; *P2, T5F, T5B, P2; rep from * to last 2 sts, K2.

Row 12: K2, *K4, P6, K4; rep from * to last 2 sts, K2.

Repeat Rows 1 through 12 for pattern.

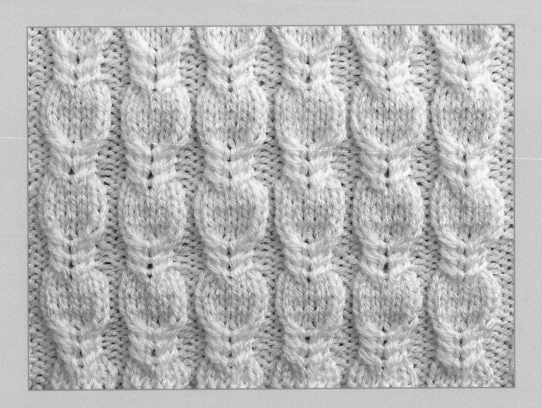

Bubble Cable

Multiple: 8 + 6

STITCH GUIDE

C3L (Cable 3 Left): Slip next st to cable needle and hold at front, K2, then K1 from cable needle.

C3R (Cable 3 Right): Slip next 2 sts to cable needle and hold at back, K1, then K2 from cable needle.

INSTRUCTIONS

Row 1 (right side): K2, P2; *K6, P2; rep from * across to last 2 sts, K2.

Row 2: K4; *P6, K2; rep from * across to last 2 sts, K2.

Row 3: Rep Row 1.

Row 4: K4; *P2, with yarn in front, sl 2, P2, K2; rep from * across to last 2 sts, K2.

Row 5: K2, P2; *C3R, C3L, P2; rep from * across to last 2 sts, K2.

Row 6: Repeat row 4.

Row 7: Repeat row 5.

Row 8: Repeat row 4.

Row 9: Repeat row 5.

Row 10: Repeat Row 2.

Row 11: Repeat Row 1.

Row 12: Repeat Row 2.

Repeat Rows 1 through 12 for pattern.

Lacy Cable Stripe

Panel: 28 sts

STITCH GUIDE

C8F: Slip next 3 sts to cable needle and hold at front, YO, P2tog, K3, then K3 from cable needle.

C8B: Slip 4 sts and YO to cable needle and hold at back, K3, YO; then from cable needle, P2tog, K3.

INSTRUCTIONS

Row 1 (right side): K2, P3, (K3, YO, P2tog) three times, K3, P3, K2.

Row 2: K5, (P3, YO, K2tog) three times, P3, K5.

Row 3: Rep Row 1.

Row 4: Rep Row 2.

Row 5: Rep Row 1.

Row 6: Rep Row 2.

Row 7: K2, P3, C8F, YO, P2tog, C8F, P3, K2.

Row 8: Rep Row 2.

Row 9: Rep Row 1.

Row 10: Rep Row 2.

Row 11: Rep Row 1.

Row 12: Rep Row 2.

Row 13: Rep Row 1.

Row 14: Rep Row 2.

Row 15: K2, P3, K3, YO, P2tog, C8B, YO, P2tog, K3, P3, K2.

Row 16: Rep Row 2.

Repeat Rows 1 through 16 for pattern.

Chubby Cables

Multiple: 17 + 4

STITCH GUIDE

C10F (Cable 10 Front): Slip next 5 sts to cable needle and hold at front, K5, then K5 from cable needle.

C10B (Cable 10 Back): Slip next 5 sts to cable needle and hold at back, K5, then K5 from cable needle.

INSTRUCTIONS

Row 1 (right side): Knit.

Row 2: K2, purl to last 2 sts, K2.

Row 3: Rep Row 1.

Row 4: Rep Row 2.

Row 5: K2; *C10F, K7; rep from * to last 2 st, K2.

Row 6: Rep Row 2.

Row 7: Rep Row 1.

Row 8: Rep Row 2.

Row 9: Rep Row 1.

Row 10: Rep Row 2.

Row 11: K2; *K5, C10B, K2; rep from * to last 2 sts, K2.

Row 12: Rep Row 2.

Repeat Rows 1 through 12 for pattern.

Cable Twist

Multiple: 16 + 4

STITCH GUIDE

C4F (Cable 4 Front): Slip next 2 sts to cable needle and hold at front, K2, then K2 from cable needle.

T4B (Twist 4 Back): Slip next 2 sts to cable needle and hold at back, K2, then P2 from cable needle.

T4F (Twist 4 Front): Slip next 2 sts to cable needle and hold in front, P2, then K2 from cable needle.

INSTRUCTIONS

Row 1 (right side): K2; *P2, C4F, P4, C4F, P2; rep from * to last 2 sts, K2.

Row 2: K2; *K2, P4, K4, P4, K2; rep from * to last 2 sts, K2.

Row 3: K2; *P2, K4, P4, K4, P2; rep from * to last 2 sts, K2.

Row 4: K2; *K2, P4, K4, P4, K2; rep from * to last 2 sts, K2.

Row 5: K2; *P2, C4F, P4, C4F, P2; rep from * to last 2 sts, K2.

Row 6: K2; *K2, P4, K4, P4, K2; rep from * to last 2 sts, K2.

Row 7: K2; *(T4B, T4F) twice; rep from * to last 2 sts, K2.

Row 8: K2; *P2, K4, P4, K4, P2; rep from * to last 2 sts, K2.

Row 9: K2; *K2, P4, C4F, P4, K2; rep from * to last 2 sts, K2.

Row 10: K2; *P2, K4, P4, K4, P2; rep from * to last 2 sts, K2.

Row 11: K2; *K2, P4, K4, P4, K2; rep from * to last 2 sts, K2.

Row 12: K2; *P2, K4, P4, K4, P2; rep from * to last 2 sts, K2.

Row 13: K2; *K2, P4, C4F, P4, K2; rep from * to last 2 sts, K2.

Row 14: K2; *P2, K4, P4, K4, P2; rep from * to last 2 sts, K2.

Row 15: K2; *K2, P4, K4, P4, K2; rep from * to last 2 sts, K2.

Row 16: K2; *P2, K4, P4, K4, P2; rep from * to last 2 sts, K2.

Row 17: K2; *K2, P4, C4F, P4, K2; rep from * to last 2 sts, K2.

Row 18: K2; *P2, K4, P4, K4, P2; rep from * to last 2 sts, K2.

Row 19: K2; *K2, P4, K4, P4, K2; rep from * to last 2 sts, K2.

Row 20: K2; *P2, K4, P4, K4, P2; rep from * to last 2 sts, K2.

Row 21: K2; *K2, P4, C4F, P4, K2; rep from * to last 2 sts, K2.

Row 22: K2; *P2, K4, P4, K4, P2; rep from * to last 2 sts, K2.

Row 23: K2; *(T4F, T4B) twice; rep from * to last 2 sts, K2.

Row 24: K2; *K2, P4, K4, P4, K2; rep from * to last 2 sts, K2.

Repeat Rows 1 through 24 for pattern.

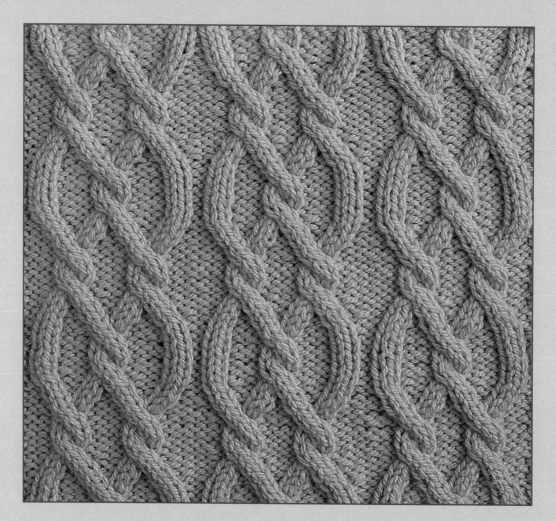

Tied Ropes

Multiple: 18 + 2

STITCH GUIDE

T3B (Twist 3 Back): Slip next st to cable needle and hold at back, K2, then P1 from cable needle.

T3F (Twist 3 Front): Slip next 2 sts to cable needle and hold at front, P1, then K2 from cable needle.

C4F (Cable 4 Front): Slip next 2 sts to cable needle and hold at front, K2, then K2 from cable needle.

INSTRUCTIONS

Row 1: P2; *K2, P4, K4, P4, K2, P2; rep from * across

Row 2: K2, P2, K4, P4, K4, P2; rep across to last 2 sts, K2.

Row 3: P2; *K2, P4, C4F, P4, K2, P2; rep from * across.

Row 4: K2, P2, K4, P4, K4, P2; rep across to last 2 sts, K2.

Row 5: P2 *(T3F, P2, T3B) twice, P2; rep from * across.

Row 6: K3, (P2, K2) three times, P2, K1; rep across to last 2 sts, K2.

Row 7: P2; *P1, T3F, T3B, P2, T3F, T3B, P3; rep from * across.

Row 8: (K4, P4) twice, K2; rep from * across to last 2 sts, K2,

Row 9: P2; *P2, (C4F, P4) twice; rep from * across.

Row 10: (K4, P4) twice, K2; rep across to last 2 sts, K2.

Row 11: P2; *P2, (K4, P4) twice; rep from * across.

Row 12: (K4, P4) twice, K2; rep from * across to last 2 sts, K2.

Row 13: P2; *P2 C4F, P4, C4F, P4; rep from * across.

Row 14: (K4, P4) twice, K2; rep across to last 2 sts, K2.

Row 15: P2; *P1, T3B, T3F, P2, T3B, T3F, P3; rep from * across.

Row 16: K3, (P2, K2) three times, P2, K1; rep across to last 2 sts, K2.

Row 17: P2; *(T3B, P2, T3F) twice, P2; rep from * across.

Row 18: K2, P2, K4, P4, K4, P2; rep cross to last 2 sts, K2.

Row 19: P2; *K2, P4, C4F, P4, K2, P2; rep from * across.

Row 20: K2, P2, K4, P4, K4, P2; rep across to last 2 sts, K2.

Repeat Rows 1 through 20 for pattern.

Framed Bobbles

Panel: 39 sts

STITCH GUIDE

C5F (Cross 5 Front): Slip next 3 sts to cable needle and hold at front, K2, slip purl st from cable needle onto left needle, P1, then K2 from cable needle.

C6B (Cable 6 Back): Slip next 3 sts to cable needle and hold at back, K3, then K3 from cable needle.

MB (Make Bobble): (K1, K1tbl, K1, K1tbl) all in same stitch.

T3B (Twist 3 Back): Slip next st to cable

needle and hold at back, K2, then P1 from cable needle.

T3F (Twist 3 Front): Slip next 2 sts to cable needle and hold at front, P1, then K2 from cable needle.

INSTRUCTIONS

Row 1 (wrong side): K2, P6, K2, P1, K3, MB, K2, P2, K1, P2, K2, MB, K3, P1, K2, P6, K2.

Row 2: P2, K6, P2, K1, P3, K4tog, P2, C5F, P2, K4tog, P3, K1, P2, K6, P2.

Row 3: K2, P6, K2, P1, K6, P2, K1, P2, K6, P1, K2, P6, K2.

Row 4: P2, C6B, P2, K1, P5, T3B, P1, T3F, P5, K1, P2, C6B, P2.

Row 5: K2, P6, K2, P1, K5, P2, K3, P2, K5, P1, K2, P6, K2.

Row 6: P2, K6, P2, K1, P4, T3B, P3, T3F, P4, K1, P2, K6, P2.

Row 7: K2, P6, K2, P1, K4, P2, K2, MB, K2, P2, K4, P1, K2, P6, K2.

Row 8: P2, K6, P2, K1, P3, T3B, P2, K4tog, P2, T3F, P3, K1, P2, K6, P2.

Row 9: K2, P6, K2, P1, K3, P2, K7, P2, K3, P1, K2, P6, K2.

Row 10: P2, K6, P2, K1, P2, T3B, P7, T3F, P2, K1, P2, K6, P2.

Row 11: K2, P6, K2, P1, K2, P2, K2, MB, K3, MB, K2, P2, K2, P1, K2, P6, K2.

Row 12: P2, C6B, P2, K1, P1, T3B, P2, K4tog, P3, K4tog, P2, T3F, P1, K1, P2, C6B, P2.

Row 13: K2, P6, K2, P1, K1, P2, K11, P2, K1, P1, K2, P6, K2.

Row 14: P2, K6, P2, K1, P1, K2, P11, K2, P1, K1, P2, K6, P2.

Row 15: K2, P6, K2, P1, K1, P2, K3, MB, K3, MB, K3, P2, K1, P1, K2, P6, K2.

Row 16: P2, K6, P2, K1, P1, T3F, P2, K4tog, P3, K4tog, P2, T3B, P1, K1, P2, K6, P2.

Row 17: K2, P6, K2, P1, K2, P2, K9, P2, K2, P1, K2, P6, K2.

Row 18: P2, K6, P2, K1, P2, T3F, P7, T3B, P2, K1, P2, K6, P2.

Row 19: K2, P6, K2, P1, K3, P2, K3, MB, K3, P2, K3, P1, K2, P6, K2.

Row 20: P2, C6B, P2, K1, P3, T3F, P2, K4tog, P2, T3B, P3, K1, P2, C6B, P2.

Row 21: K2, P6, K2, P1, K4, P2, K5, P2, K4, P1, K2, P6, K2.

Row 22: P2, K6, P2, K1, P4, T3F, P3, T3B, P4, K1, P2, K6, P2.

Row 23: K2, P6, K2, P1, K5, P2, K3, P2, K5, P1, K2, P6, K2.

Row 24: P2, K6, P2, K1, P5, T3F, P1, T3B, P5, K1, P2, K6, P2.

Repeat Rows 1 through 24 for pattern.

Cable Columns

Multiple: 16 + 6

STITCH GUIDE

T2 (Twist 2): Inserting needle from front of work, knit 2nd st on left needle through back lp, but do not remove from needle; knit first st on left needle; slip both sts off together.

C10F (Cable 10 Front): Slip next 5 sts to cable needle and hold at front, K5, then K5 from cable needle.

INSTRUCTIONS

Row 1 (wrong side): *K2, P2, K2, P10; rep from * to last 6 sts, K2, P2, K2.

Row 2: *P2, T2, P2, K10; rep from * to last 6 sts, P2, T2, P2.

Row 3: *K2, P2, K2, P10; rep from * to last 6 sts, K2, P2, K2.

Row 4: *P2, T2, P2, K10; rep from * to last 6 sts, P2, T2, P2.

Row 5: *K2, P2, K2, P10; rep from * to last 6 sts, K2, P2, K2.

Row 6: *P2, T2, P2, K10; rep from * to last 6 sts, P2, T2, P2.

Row 7: *K2, P2, K2, P10; rep from * to last 6 sts, K2, P2, K2.

Row 8: *P2, T2, P2, K10; rep from * to last 6 sts, P2, T2, P2.

Row 9: *K2, P2, K2, P10; rep from * to last 6 sts, K2, P2, K2.

Row 10: *P2, T2, P2, K10; rep from * to last 6 sts, P2, T2, P2.

Row 11: *K2, P2, K2, P10; rep from * to last 6 sts, K2, P2, K2.

Row 12: *P2, T2, P2, C10; rep from * to last 6 sts, P2, T2, P2.

Repeat Rows 1 through 12 for pattern.

Desert Sand
Multiple: 12 + 4

STITCH GUIDE

C6F (Cable 6 Front): Slip next 3 sts to cable needle and hold at front, K3, then K3 from cable needle.

C6B (Cable 6 Back): Slip next 3 sts to cable needle and hold at back, K3, then K3 from cable needle.

INSTRUCTIONS

Row 1 (right side): Knit.

Row 2: K2, purl to last 2 sts, K2.

Row 3: K2; *C6F, K6; rep from * to last 2 sts, K2.

Row 4: K2, purl to last 2 sts, K2.

Row 5: Knit.

Row 6: K2, purl to last 2 sts, K2.

Row 7: K2; *K6, C6B; rep from * to last 2 sts, K2.

Row 8: K2, purl to last 2 sts, K2.

Repeat Rows 3 through 8 for pattern.

Chain Link Cable

Panel: 29 sts

STITCH GUIDE

T5B (Twist 5 Back): Slip next 2 sts to cable needle and hold at back, K3, then P2 from cable needle.

T5F (Twist 5 Front): Slip next 3 sts onto cable needle and hold at front, P2, K3 from cable needle.

C6F (Cable 6 Front): Slip next 3 sts to cable needle and hold at front, K3, then K3 from cable needle.

C6B (Cable 6 Back): Slip next 3 sts to cable needle and hold at back, K3, then K3 from cable needle.

INSTRUCTIONS

Row 1 (right side): P2, K3, P6, K3, P1, K3, P6, K3, P2.

Row 2: K2, P3, K6, P3, K1, P3, K6, P3, K2.

Row 3: Rep Row 1.

Row 4: Rep Row 2.

Row 5: P2, T5F, P4, K3, P1, K3, P4, T5B, P2.

Row 6: K4, P3, K4, P3, K1, P3, K4, P3, K4.

Row 7: P4, T5F, P2, K3, P1, K3, P2, T5B, P4.

Row 8: K6, P3, K2, P3, K1, P3, K2, P3, K6.

Row 9: P6, T5F, K3, P1, K3, T5B, P6.

Row 10: K8, P6, K1, P6, K8.

Row 11: P8, C6B, P1, C6F, P8.

Row 12: K8, P6, K1, P6, K8.

Row 13: P8, K6, P1, K6, P8.

Row 14: Rep Row 12.

Row 15: Rep Row 13.

Row 16: Rep Row 12.

Row 17: P8, C6B, P1, C6F, P8.

Row 18: Rep Row 10.

Row 19: P6, T5B, K3, P1, K3, T5F, P6.

Row 20: Rep Row 8.

Row 21: P4, T5B, P2, K3, P1, K3, P2, T5F, P4.

Row 22: Rep Row 6.

Row 23: P2, T5B, P4, K3, P1, K3, P4, T5F, P2.

Row 24: Rep Row 2.

Repeat Rows 1 through 24 for pattern.

C4L (Cross 4 Left): Slip next st to cable needle and hold at front, P3, then K1 from cable needle.

C4R (Cross 4 Right): (Sl 3 sts to cable needle and hold at back, K1, then P3 from cable needle.

INSTRUCTIONS

Row 1: P3, K4, P6, K4, P3.

Row 2 (right side): K3, P4, C4B, K2, P4, K3.

Row 3: P3, K4, P6, K4, P3.

Row 4: K3, P4, K2, C4F, P4, K3.

Rows 5 through 20: Repeat Rows 1 through 4.

Row 21: P3, K4, P6, K4, P3.

Row 22: K3, P4, K6, P4, K3.

Row 23: P3, K3, C4L, C4R, K3, P3.

Row 24: K3, P3, K3, P2, K3, P3, K3.

Row 25: P3, K2, C4L, K2, C4R, K2, P3.

Row 26: K3, P2, K3, P4, K3, P2, K3.

Row 27: P3, K1, C4L, K4, C4R, K1, P3.

Row 28: K3, P1, K3, P6, K3, P1, K3.

Row 29: P3, K1, P3, K6, P3, K1, P3.

Row 30: K3, P1, K3, P6, K3, P1, K3.

Row 31: P3, K1, P3, K6, P3, K1, P3.

Row 32: K3, P1, K3, P6, K3, P1, K3.

Row 33: P3, K1, C4R, K4, C4L, K1, P3.

Row 34: K3, P2, K3, P4, K3, P2, K3.

Row 35: P3, K2, C4R, K2, C4L, K2, P3.

Row 36: K3, P3, K3, P2, K3, P3, K3.

Row 37: P3, K3, C4R, C4L, K3, P3.

Row 38: K3, P4, K6, P4, K3.

Repeat Rows 1 through 38 for complete pattern, ending with Row 20 to complete motif.

Braided Cable

Panel: 20 sts

STITCH GUIDE

C4F (Cable 4 Front): Slip next 2 sts to cable needle and hold at front, K2, then K2 from cable needle.

C4B (Cable 4 Back): Slip next 2 sts to cable needle and hold at back, K2, then K2 from cable needle.

Bobbles and Diamonds

Panel: 17 sts

STITCH GUIDE

T3B (Twist 3 Back): Slip next st to cable needle and hold at back, K2, then P1 from cable needle.

T3F (Twist 3 Front): Slip next 2 sts to cable needle and hold at front, P1, then K2 from cable needle.

C5B (Cross 5 Back): Slip next 3 sts to cable needle and hold at back, K2, then slip purl st from cable needle back to left needle and purl it, then K2 from cable needle.

BB (Bobble): [(K1, P1) twice, K1 all in next st], turn; P5, turn; K5, pass 4th, 3rd, 2nd, and first st separately over the last st knitted.

INSTRUCTIONS

Row 1(wrong side): K6, P2, K1, P2, K6.

Row 2: P6, C5B, P6.

Row 3: K6, P2, K1, P2, K6.

Row 4: P5, T3B, K1, T3F, P5.

Row 5: K5, P2, K1, P1, K1, P2, K5.

Row 6: P4, T3B, K1, P1, K1, T3F, P4.

Row 7: K4, P2, (K1, P1) twice, K1, P2, K4.

Row 8: P3, T3B, (K1, P1) twice, K1, T3F, P3.

Row 9: K3, P2, K1, (P1, K1) 3 times, P2, K3.

Row 10: P2, T3B, (K1, P1) 3 times, K1, T3F, P2.

Row 11: K2, P2, (K1, P1) 5 times, P1, K2.

Row 12: P2, T3F, (P1, K1) 3 times, P1, T3B, P2.

Row 13: K3, P2, (K1, P1) 3 times, K1, P2, K3.

Row 14: P3, T3F, (P1, K1) twice, P1, T3B, P3.

Row 15: K4, P2, (K1, P1) twice, K1, P2, K4.

Row 16: P4, T3F, P1, K1, P1, T3B, P4.

Row 17: K5, P2, K1, P1, K1, P2, K5.

Row 18: P5, T3F, P1, T3B, P5.

Row 19: K6, P2, K1, P2, K6.

Row 20: P6, C5B, P6.

Row 21: K6, P2, K1, P2, K6.

Row 22: P5, T3B, P1, T3F, P5.

Row 23: K5, P2, K3, P2, K5.

Row 24: P4, T3B, P3, T3F, P4.

Row 25: K4, P2, K5, P2, K4.

Row 26: P4, K2, P2, BB, P2, K2, P4.

Row 27: K4, P2, K5, P2, K4.

Row 28: P4, T3F, P3, T3B, P4.

Row 29: K5, P2, K3, P2, K5.

Row 30: P5, T3F, P1, T3B, P5.

Repeat Rows 1 through 30 for pattern.

43

Popcorn Cables
Panel: 32

STITCH GUIDE:

C4B (Cable 4 Back): Slip next 2 sts to cable needle and hold at back, K2, then K2 from cable needle.

T4B (Twist 4 Back): Slip next 2 sts to cable needle and hold at back, K2, then P2 from cable needle.

T4F (Twist 4 Front): Slip next 2 sts to cable needle and hold in front, P2, then K2 from cable needle.

PC (Popcorn): (P1, K1) twice in next st; lift 2nd, 3rd and 4th sts over first st.

INSTRUCTIONS

Row 1 (right side): K2, P2, K2, P8, C4B, P8, K2, P2, K2.

Row 2: K4, P2, K8, P4, K8, P2, K4.

Row 3: K2, P2, (T4F, P4, T4B) twice, P2, K2.

Row 4: K6, (P2, K4) 3 times, P2, K6.

Row 5: K2, P4, (T4F, T4B, P4) twice, K2.

Row 6: (K8, P4) twice, K8.

Row 7: K2, P6, C4B, P3, PC (twice), P3, C4B, P6, K2.

Row 8: (K8, P4) twice, K8.

Row 9: K2, P4, (T4B, T4F, P4) twice, K2.

Row 10: K6, (P2, K4) 4 times, K2.

Row 11: K2, P2, (T4B, P4, T4F) twice, P2, K2.

Row 12: K4, P2, K8, P4, K8, P2, K4.

Row 13: K2, P2, K2, P3, (PC) twice, P3, C4B, P3, (PC) twice, P3, K2, P2, K2.

Row 14: K4, P2, K8, P4, K8, P2, K4.

Repeat Rows 1 through 14 for pattern.

Blarney Kiss

Panel: 20 sts

STITCH GUIDE

C4F (Cable 4 Front): Slip next 2 sts to cable needle and hold at front, K2, then K2 from cable needle.

C4B (Cable 4 Back): Slip next 2 sts to cable needle and hold at back, K2, then K2 from cable needle.

INSTRUCTIONS

Row 1 (right side): K2, P2, K2, C4B, C4F, K2, P2, K2.

Row 2 and all even rows: K4, P12, K4.

Row 3: K2, P2, C4B, K4, C4F, P2, K2.

Row 5: K2, P2, K2, C4B, C4F, K2, P2, K2.

Row 7: K2, P2, C4B, K4, C4F, P2, K2.

Row 9: K2, P2, C4F, K4, C4B, P2, K2.

Row 11: K2, P2, K2, C4F, C4B, K2, P2, K2.

Row 13: K2, P2, C4F, K4, C4B, P2, K2.

Row 15: K2, P2, K2, C4F, C4B, K2, P2, K2.

Row 16: K4, P12, K4.

Repeat Rows 1 through 16 for pattern.

Trellis

Multiple: 8 + 4, having at least 20 sts.

STITCH GUIDE

Tw2F (Twist 2 front): Knit into front of second st, on left needle, but do not remove from needle; then knit into front of first stitch on left needle and slip both sts off needle together.

Tw2B (Twist 2 back): Knit into back of second st on left needle, but do not remove from needle, then reaching behind work, knit into back of first stitch on left needle and slip both sts off needle together.

INSTRUCTIONS

Row 1 (right side): K2, P7; *Tw2F, P6; rep from * to last 3 sts, P1, K2.

Row 2: K9; *P2, K6; rep from * to last 3 sts, K3.

Row 3: K2;*Tw2B, P4, Tw2F; rep from * to last 2 sts, K2.

Row 4: K2; *P2, K4, P2; rep from * to last 2 sts, K2.

Row 5: K2;*K1, Tw2B, P2, Tw2F, K1; rep from * to last 2 sts, K2.

Row 6: K2; *P3, K2, P3; rep from * to last 2 sts, K2.

Row 7: K2;*K2, Tw2B, Tw2F, K2; rep from * to last 2 sts, K2.

Row 8: K2; *K3, P2, K3; rep from * to last 2 sts, K2.

Row 9: K2; *P3, Tw2F, P3; rep from * to last 2 sts, K2.

Row 10: K2; *K3, P2, K3; rep from * to last 2 sts, K2.

Row 11: K2; *P2, Tw2F, Tw2B, P2; rep from * to last 2 sts, K2.

Row 12: K2; *K2, P4, K2; rep from * to last 2 sts, K2.

Row13: K2; *P1, Tw2F, K2, Tw2B, P1; rep from * to last 2 sts, K2.

Row 14: K2; *K1, P6, K1; rep from * to last 2 sts, K2.

Row 15: K2; *Tw2F, K4, Tw2B; rep from * to last 2 sts, K2.

Row 16: K2; *P1, K6, P1; rep from * to last 2 sts, K2.

Repeat Rows 1 through 16 for pattern.

Two-Tone Cable

Multiple: 12 + 4

STITCH GUIDE

MC: Main color

CC: Contrast color

Note: *Use MC except where CC is indicated.*

Note: *To make it easier to work with two colors at a time, wind the CC color around bobbins and work with the bobbins rather than with two balls of yarn. When changing colors, always bring the new color up from under the old color to prevent holes in the knitting.*

T6L (Twist 6 Left): Sl 4 sts to cable needle and hold at front, K2CC sts; then K2MC sts and K2CC sts from cable needle.

INSTRUCTIONS

Row 1 (right side): K2 with MC: *K2, P2, K2CC, K2, K2CC, P2; rep from * to last 2 sts, K2.

Row 2 (and all even rows): Work all stitches with same color as used on row below, working as follows: K2; *K2, P6, K2, P2; rep from * to last 2 sts, K2.

Row 3: Rep Row 1.

Row 5: K2 with MC; *K2 , P2, T6L, P2; rep from * to last 2 sts, K2.

Row 7: Rep Row 1.

Row 8: Rep Row 2.

Repeat Rows 1 through 8 for pattern.

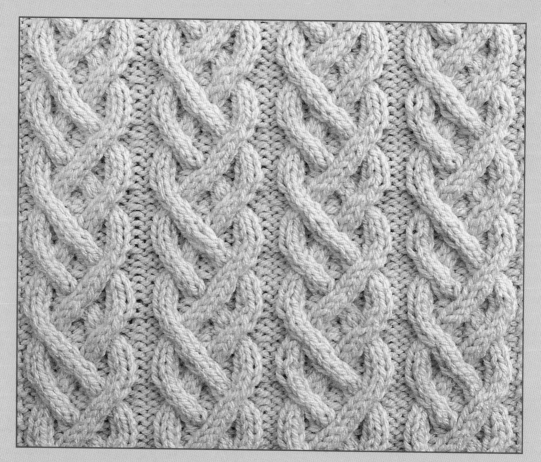

Twining Vines

Multiple: 15 + 4

STITCH GUIDE:

C4F (Cable 4 Front): Slip next 2 sts to cable needle and hold at front, K2, then K2 from cable needle.

C4B (Cable 4 Back): Slip next 2 sts to cable needle and hold at back, K2, then K2 from cable needle.

T3B (Twist 3 Back): Slip next st to cable needle and hold at back, K2, then P1 from cable needle.

T3F (Twist 3 Front): Slip next 2 sts to cable needle and hold at front, P1, then K2 from cable needle.

T5B (Twist 5 Back): Slip next 3 sts to cable needle and hold at back, K2, slip purl stitch from cable needle onto left-hand needle, P1, then K2 from cable needle.

T5F (Twist 5 Front): Slip next 3 sts to cable needle and hold in front, K2, slip purl stitch from cable needle onto left-hand needle, P1, then K2 from cable needle.

INSTRUCTIONS

Row 1: K2; *K1, P2, K2, P2, K1, P2, K2, P2, K1; rep from * to last 2 sts, K2.

Row 2 (right side): K2; *P1, K2, P2, TF5, P2, K2, P1; rep from * to last 2 sts, K2.

Row 3: K2; *K1, P2, K2, P2, K1, P2, K2, P2, K1; rep from * to last 2 sts, K2.

Row 4: K2; *P1, T3F, T3B, P1, T3F, T3B, P1; rep from * to last 2 sts, K2.

Row 5: K2; *K2, P4, K3, P4, K2; rep from * to last 2 sts, K2.

Row 6: K2; *P2, C4B, P3, C4F, P2; rep from * to last 2 sts, K2.

Row 7: K2; *K2, P4, K3, P4, K2; rep from * to last 2 sts, K2.

Row 8: K2; *P1, T3B, T3F, P1, T3B, T3F, P1; rep from * to last 2 sts, K2.

Row 9: K2; *K1, P2, K2, P2, K1, P2, K2, P2, K1; rep from * to last 2 sts, K2.

Row 10: K2; *P1, K2, P2, T5B, P2, K2, P1; rep from * to last 2 sts, K2.

Row 11: K2; *K1, P2, K2, P2, K1, P2, K2, P2, K1; rep from * to last 2 sts, K2.

Row 12: K2; *P1, T3F, T3B, P1, T3F, T3B, P1; rep from * to last 2 sts, K2.

Row 13: K2; *K2, P4, K3, P4, K2; rep from * to last 2 sts, K2.

Row 14: K2; *P2, C4B, P3, C4F, P2; rep from * to last 2 sts, K2.

Row 15: K2; *K2, P4, K3, P4, K2; rep from * to last 2 sts, K2.

Row 16: K2; *P1, T3B, T3F, P1, T3B, T3F, P1; rep from * to last 2 sts, K2.

Row 17: K2; *K1, P2, K2, P2, K1, P2, K2, P2, K1; rep from * to last 2 sts, K2.

Repeat Rows 2 through 17 for pattern.

Cable and Cable

Panel: 42 sts

STITCH GUIDE

C4F (Cable 4 Front): Slip next 2 sts to cable needle and hold at front, K2, then K2 from cable needle.

C4B (Cable 4 Back): Slip next 2 sts to cable needle and hold at back, K2, then K2 from cable needle.

C6B (Cable 6 Back): Slip next 3 sts to cable needle and hold at back, K3, then K3 from cable needle.

T4B (Twist 4 Back): Slip next 2 sts to cable needle and hold at back, K2, then P2 from cable needle.

T4F (Twist 4 Front): Slip next 2 sts to cable needle and hold in front, P2, then K2 from cable needle.

T3B (Twist 3 Back): Slip next st to cable needle and hold at back, K2, then P1 from cable needle.

T3F (Twist 3 Front): Slip next 2 sts to cable needle and hold at front, P1, then K2 from cable needle.

INSTRUCTIONS

Row 1 (right side): K8, P8, C4B, K2, C4F, P8, K8.

Row 2: K2, P6, K8, P10, K8, P6, K2.

Row 3: K2, C6B, P6, T4B, K2, C4B, T4F, P6, C6B, K2.

Row 4: K2, P6, K6, P2, K2, P6, K2, P2, K6, P6, K2.

Row 5: K8, P4, T4B, P1, T3B, K2, T3F, P1, T4F, P4, K8.

Row 6: K2, P6, K4, P2, K3, P2, K1, P2, K1, P2, K3, P2, K4, P6, K2.

Row 7: K2, C6B, P2, T4B, P2, T3B, P1, K2, P1, T3F, P2, T4F, P2, C6B, K2.

Row 8: K2, P6, K2, P2, K4, (P2, K2) twice, P2, K4, P2, K2, P6, K2.

Row 9: K8, P2, K2, P3, T3B, P2, K2, P2, T3F, P3, K2, P2, K8.

Row 10: K2, P6, K2, (P2, K3) 4 times, P2, K2, P6, K2.

Row 11: K2, C6B, P2, T4F, T3B, P3, K2, P3, T3F, T4B, P2, C6B, K2.

Row 12: K2, P6, K4, P4, K4, P2, K4, P4, K4, P6, K2.

Row 13: K8, P4, C4B, P4, K2, P4, C4F, P4, K8.

Row 14: K2, P6, K4, P4, K4, P2, K4, P4, K4, P6, K2.

Row 15: K2, C6B, P2, T4B, T4F, P2, K2, P2, T4B, T4F, P2, C6B, K2.

Row 16: K2, P6, K2, P2, K4, (P2, K2) twice, P2, K4, P2, K2, P6, K2.

Row 17: K8, P2, K2, P4, T4F, K2, T4B, P4, K2, P2, K8.

Row 18: K2, P6, K2, P2, K6, P6, K6, P2, K2, P6, K2.

Row 19: K2, C6B, P2, T4F, P4, C4F, K2, P4, T4B, P2, C6B, K2.

Row 20: K2, P6, K4, P2, K4, P6, K4, P2, K4, P6, K2.

Row 21: K8, P4, T4F, P2, K2, C4B, P2, T4B, P4, K8.

Row 22: K2, P6, K6, P2, K2, P6, K2, P2, K6, P6, K2.

Row 23: K2, C6B, P6, T4F, C4F, K2, T4B, P6, C6B, K2.

Row 24: K2, P6, K8, P10, K8, P6, K2.

Repeat Rows 1 through 24 for pattern.

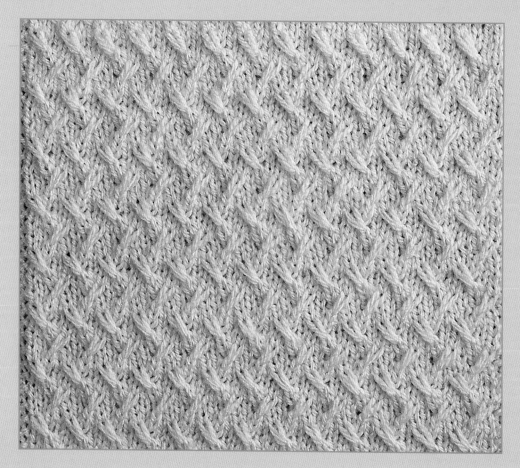

Scattered Oats

Multiple: 4 + 9

STITCH GUIDE

C3L (Cable 3 Left): Slip next st to cable needle and hold at front, K2, then K1 from cable needle.

C3R (Cable 3 Right): Slip next 2 sts to cable needle and hold at back, K1, then K2 from cable needle.

INSTRUCTIONS

Row 1 (right side): K4; *yb, sl 1 as to purl, K3; rep from * to last st, K1.

Row 2: K2, P2; *yf, sl 1 as to purl, P3; rep from * to last 5 sts, sl 1, P2, K2.

Row 3: K2; *C3R, K1; rep from * to last 3 sts, K3.

Row 4: K2, purl to last 2 sts, K2.

Row 5: Rep Row 1.

Row 6: Rep Row 2.

Row 7: K3; *K1, C3L; rep from * to last 2 sts, K2.

Row 8: K2, purl to last 2 sts. K2.

Repeat Rows 1 through 8 for pattern.

Quilted Cables

Multiple: 8 + 6

STITCH GUIDE

C4F (Cable 4 Front): Slip next 2 sts to cable needle and hold at front, K2, then K2 from cable needle.

C4B (Cable 4 Back): Slip next 2 sts to cable needle and hold at back, K2, then K2 from cable needle.

INSTRUCTIONS

Row 1 (wrong side): K2, purl to last 2 sts, K2.

Row 2: P2, K2, *C4F; rep from * to last 2 sts, P2.

Row 3: K2, purl to last 2 sts, K2.

Row 4: P2, *C4B rep from * to last 4 sts, K2, P2.

Repeat Rows 1 through 4 for pattern.

Entwined Lozenges

Panel: 32 sts

STITCH GUIDE

C4B (Cable 4 Back): Slip next 2 sts to cable needle and hold at back, K2, then K2 from cable needle.

T3B (Twist 3 Back): Slip next st to cable needle and hold at back, K2, then P1 from cable needle.

T3F (Twist 3 Front): Slip next 2 sts to cable needle and hold at front, P1, then K2 from cable needle.

Tw2K: Knit into 2nd st, on left needle, but do not remove from needle; then knit into first stitch on left needle and slip both sts off needle together.

Tw2P: Purl into 2nd st on left needle, but do not remove from needle, then purl into first stitch on left needle and slip both sts off needle together.

INSTRUCTIONS

Row 1 (right side): K2, P2, Tw2K, P2, K2, P4, K4, P4, K2, P2, Tw2K, P2, K2.

Row 2: K4, Tw2P, K2, P2, K4, P4, K4, P2, K2, Tw2P, K4.

Row 3: K2, P2, Tw2K, P2, K2, P4, C4B, P4, K2, P2, Tw2K, P2, K2.

Row 4: K4, Tw2P, K2, P2, K4, P4, K4, P2, K2, Tw2P, K4.

Row 5: K2, P2, Tw2K, P2, (T3F, P2, T3B) twice, P2, Tw2K, P2, K2.

Row 6: K4, Tw2P, K3, (P2, K2) 3 times, P2, K3, Tw2P, K4.

Row 7: K2, P2, Tw2K, P3, T3F, T3B, P2, T3F, T3B, P3, Tw2K, P2, K2.

Row 8: K4, Tw2P, (K4, P4) twice, K4, Tw2P, K4.

Row 9: K2, P2, Tw2K, P4, C4B, P4, C4B, P4, Tw2K, P2, K2.

Row 10: K4, Tw2P, (K4, P4) twice, K4, Tw2P, K4.

Row 11: K2, P2, Tw2K, (P4, K4) twice, P4, Tw2K, P2, K2.

Row 12: K4, Tw2P, (K4, P4) twice, K4, Tw2P, K4.

Row 13: K2, P2, Tw2K, P4, (C4B, P4) twice, Tw2K, P2, K2.

Row 14: K4, Tw2P, (K4, P4) twice, K4, Tw2P, K4.

Row 15: K2, P2, Tw2K, P3, T3B, T3F, P2, T3B, T3F, P3, Tw2K, P2, K2.

Row 16: K4, Tw2P, K3, (P2, K2) 3 times, P2, K3, Tw2P, K4.

Row 17: K2, P2, Tw2K, P2, T3B, P2, T3F, T3B, P2, T3F, P2, Tw2K, P2, K2.

Row 18: K4, Tw2P, K2, P2, K4, P4, K4, P2, K2, Tw2P, K4.

Row 19: K2, P2, Tw2K, P2, K2, P4, C4B, P4, K2, P2, Tw2K, P2, K2.

Row 20: K4, Tw2P, K2, P2, K4, P4, K4, P2, K2, Tw2P, K4.

Repeat Rows 1 through 20 for pattern.

Lacy Cables

Multiple: 20 + 4

STITCH GUIDE

C4F (Cable 4 Front): Slip next 2 sts to cable needle and hold at front, K2, then K2 from cable needle.

C4B (Cable 4 Back): Slip next 2 sts to cable needle and hold at back, K2, then K2 from cable needle.

INSTRUCTIONS

Row 1 (right side): K1; *P2, K8, P2, K8; rep from * to last 3 sts, P2, K1.

Row 2 and all even rows: K3; *P8, k2; rep from * to last st, K1.

Row 3: K1; *P2, K8, P2, K1, (sl 1, K1, PSSO, YO) 3 times, K1; rep from * to last 3 sts, P2, K1.

Row 5: K1; *P2, K8, P2, (sl 1, K1, PSSO, YO) 3 times, K2; rep from * to last 3 sts, P2, K1.

Row 7: K1; *P2, K8, P2, K1, (sl 1, K1, PSSO, YO) twice, K3: rep from * to last 3 sts, P2, K1.

Row 9: K1, P2; *C4B, C4F, P2; rep from * to last st, K1.

Row 11: K1; *P2, K1, (sl 1, K1, PSSO, YO) 3 times, K1, P2, K8; rep from * to last 3 sts, P2, K1.

Row 13: K1; *P2, (sl 1, K1, PSSO, YO) 3 times, K2, P2, K8; rep from * to last 3 sts, P2, K1.

Row 15: K1; *P2, K1, (sl 1, K1, PSSO, YO) twice, K3, P2, K8; rep from * to last 3 sts, P2, K1.

Row 17: K1, P2; *C4B, C4F, P2; rep from * to last st, K1.

Row 18: K3; *P8, k2; rep from * to last st, K1.

Repeat Rows 3 through 18 for pattern.

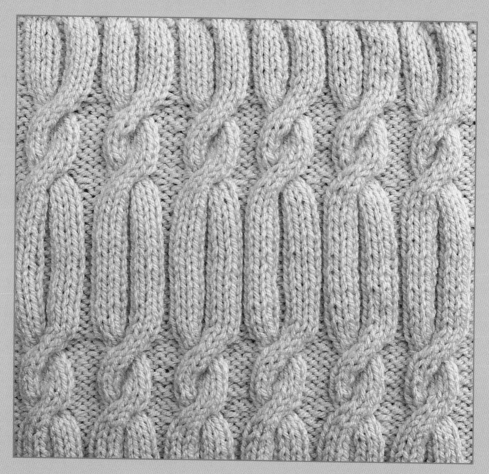

Cable Rows

Multiple: 10 + 6

STITCH GUIDE

T4B: Slip 1 st to cable needle and hold at back, K3, then P1 from cable needle.

T4F: Slip 3 sts to cable needle and hold in front, P1, K3 from cable needle.

C6B: Slip 3 sts to cable needle and hold at back, K3, then K3 from cable needle.

INSTRUCTIONS

Row 1 (right side): K2; *(P2, K3) twice; rep from * to last 4 sts, P2, K2.

Row 2: K2; *(K2, P3) twice; rep from * to last 4 sts, K4.

Rows 3 through 8: Rep Rows 1 and 2 three times.

Row 9: K2; *P2, T4F, T4B; rep from * to last 4 sts, P2, K2.

Row 10: K2; *K3, P6, K1; rep from * to last 4 sts. K4.

Row 11: K2; *P3, C6B, P1; rep from * to last 4 sts, P2, K2.

Row 12: Rep Row 10.

Row 13: K2; *P3, K6, P1; rep from * to last 4 sts, P2, K2.

Rows 14 through 17: Rep Rows 10 and 13 twice.

Row 18: Rep Row 10.

Row 19: Rep Row 11.

Row 20: Rep Row 10.

Row 21: K2; *P2, T4B, T4F; rep from * to last 4 sts, P2, K2.

Row 22: Rep Row 2.

Rows 23 through 30: Rep Rows 1 and 2 four times.

Repeat Rows 1 through 30 for pattern.

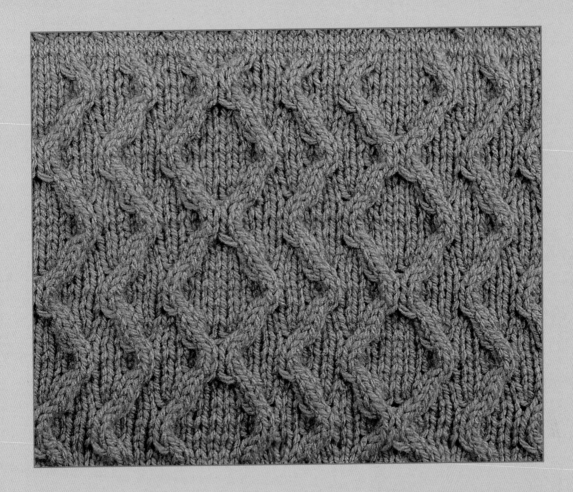

Zig-Zag Cables

Multiple: 36 + 2

STITCH GUIDE

C4F (Cable 4 Front): Slip next 2 sts to cable needle and hold at front, K2, then K2 from cable needle.

C4B (Cable 4 Back): Slip next 2 sts to cable needle and hold at back, K2, then K2 from cable needle.

INSTRUCTIONS

Row 1(wrong side): K1, purl to last st, K1.

Row 2: Knit.

Row 3 and all odd rows: K1, purl to last st, K1.

Row 4: K1; *(K2, C4F) 3 times, (C4B, K2) 3 times; rep from * to last st, K1.

Row 6: Knit.

Row 8: K1; *(K2, C4B) 3 times, (C4F, K2) 3 times; rep from * to last st, K1.

Row 10: Knit.

Row 12: K1; *(C4B, K2) 2 times, C4B, K4, (C4F, K2) twice, C4F; rep from * to last st, K1.

Row 14: Knit.

Row 16: K1; *(C4F, K2) twice, C4F, K4, (C4B, K2) twice, C4B; rep from * to last st, K1.

Row 18: Knit.

Row 19: K1; purl to last st, K1.

Repeat Rows 4 through 19 for pattern.

Cable Crossing

Panel: 27 sts

STITCH GUIDE

C7B (Cable 7 Back): Sl 4 sts to cable needle and hold in back, K3, sl 1 purl st from cable needle to left hand needle and P1, K3 from cable needle.

C7F (Cable 7 Front): Sl 4 sts to cable needle and hold in front, K3, sl 1 purl st from cable needle to left hand needle, P1, K3 from cable needle.

INSTRUCTIONS

Row 1 (right side): K5, (P1, K3) 4 times, P1, K5.

Row 2: K1, (K1, P3) 6 times, K2.

Row 3: Rep Row 1.

Row 4: K2, (P3, K1) 6 times, K1.

Row 5: K5, P1, K3, P1, C7F, P1, K3, P1, K5.

Row 6: K2, (P3, K1) 6 times, K1.

Row 7: Rep Row 1.

Row 8: Rep Row 4.

Row 9: K5, P1, (C7B, P1) twice, K5.

Row 10: Rep Row 4.

Row 11: Rep Row 1.

Row 12: Rep Row 4.

Row 13: K2, (C7F, P1) twice, C7F, K2.

Row 14: Rep Row2.

Row 15: Rep Row 1.

Row 16: Rep Row 4.

Row 17: Rep Row 9.

Row 18: Rep Row 4.

Row 19: Rep Row 1.

Row 20: Rep Row 2.

Row 21: Rep Row 5.

Row 22: Rep Row 6.

Repeat Rows 1 through 22 for pattern.

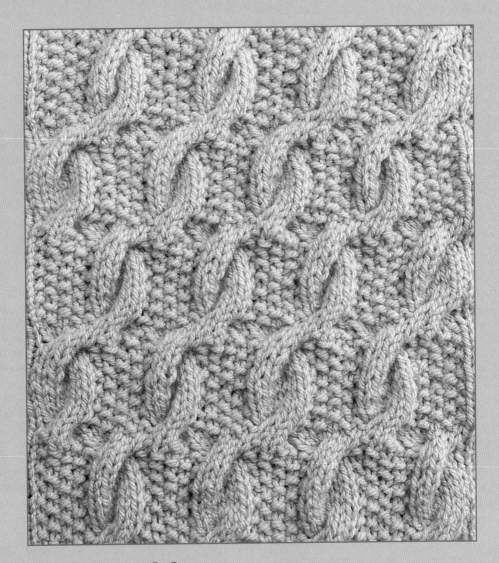

Marching Cables

Multiple: 11+ 6

STITCH GUIDE

C6B (Cable 6 Back): Slip next 3 sts to cable needle and hold at back, K3, then K3 from cable needle.

INSTRUCTIONS

Row 1 (right side): K3; *K6, (K1, P1,) twice, K1; rep from * across to last 3 sts, K3

Row 2: K2, P1, *(K1, P1) twice, K1, P6; rep from * across to last 3 sts, P1, K2.

Row 3: K3; *C6B, (K1, P1) twice, K1; rep from * across to last 3 sts, K3.

Rows 4 through 11: Rep Rows 2 and 1.

Row 12: Rep Row 2.

Row 13: Rep Row 3.

Row 14: Rep Row 2.

Row 15: K3; *(K1, P1) twice, K7; rep from * across to last 3 sts, K3.

Row 16: K2, P1; *P6, (K1, P1) twice, K1; rep from * across to last 3 sts, P1, K2.

Row 17: K3; *(K1, P1) twice, K1, C6B; rep from * across to last 3 sts, K3.

Row 18 through 26: Rep Rows 15 and 16 .

Row 27: Rep Row 17.

Row 28: Rep Row 16.

Repeat Rows 1 through 28 for pattern.

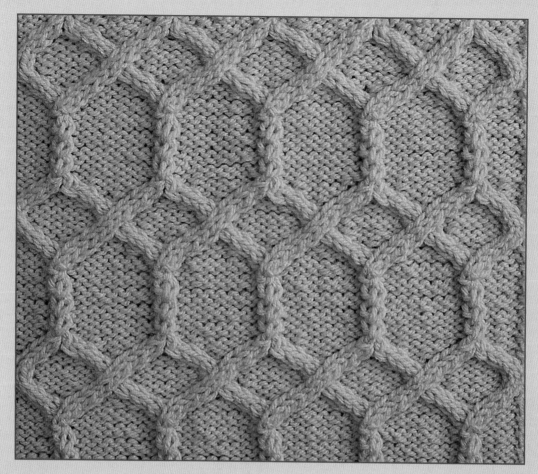

Hexagons and Diamonds

Multiple: 10 + 2

STITCH GUIDE

T2 (Twist 2): Inserting needle from front of work, knit 2nd st on left needle through back lp, but do not remove from needle; knit first st on left needle; slip both sts off together.

C4B (Cable 4 Back): Slip next 2 sts to cable needle and hold at back, K2, then K2 from cable needle.

T4B (Twist 4 Back): Slip next 2 sts to cable needle and hold at back, K2, then P2 from cable needle.

T4F (Twist 4 Front): Slip next 2 sts to cable needle and hold in front, P2, then K2 from cable needle.

C4B (Back Cross): Sl 2 sts to Cable needle and hold at back, K2, then K2 from cable needle.

INSTRUCTIONS

Row 1 (right side): P5, *T2, P8; rep from *, ending with T2, P5.

Row 2: K5, *P2, K8; rep from *, ending with P2, K5.

Row 3: P5, *T2, P8; rep from *, ending with T2, P5.

Row 4: K5, *P2, K8; rep from *, ending with P2, K5.

Row 5: P5, *T2, P8; rep from *, ending with T2, P5.

Row 6: K5, *P2, K8; rep from *, ending with P2, K5.

Row 7: P5, *T2, P8; rep from *, ending with T2, P5.

Row 8: K5, *purl into the front and back of each of the next 2 sts (4 sts worked in 2 sts), K8; rep from * ending last repeat with K5.

Row 9: P5; *C4B, P8; rep from *, ending with C4B, P5.

Row 10: K5, *P4, K8; rep from *, ending with P4, K5.

Row 11: P3, *T4B, T4F, P4; rep from *, ending last rep with P3.

Row 12: K3; *P2, K4, rep from *, ending last rep with P2, K3.

Row 13: P1, *T4B, P4, T4F; rep from *, ending with P1.

Row 14: K1, P2; *K8, P4; rep from *, ending last rep with K8, P2, K1.

Row 15: P1, K2; *P8, C4B; rep from *, ending with P8, K2, P1.

Row 16: Repeat Row 14.

Row 17: P1; *T4F, P4, T4B, rep from *, ending with P1.

Row 18: Repeat Row 12.

Row 19: P3; *T4F, T4B, P4; rep from *, ending last rep with P3.

Row 20: K5; *(P2tog) twice, K8; rep fom *, ending last rep with K5.

Repeat Rows 1 through 20 for pattern.

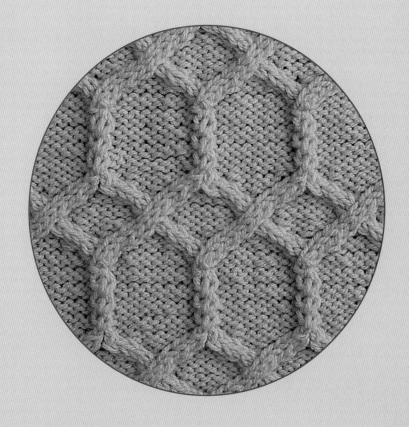

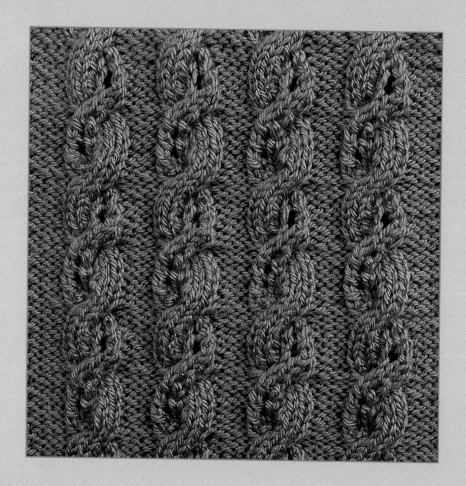

Cables with Lace

Multiple: 11 + 8

STITCH GUIDE

C7B (Cable 7 Back): Sl 4 sts on cable needle and hold in back, K3, then K4 from cable needle.

INSTRUCTIONS

Row 1 (right side): K2, P4; *K2tog, YO, K1, YO, sl 1, K1, PSSO, K2, P4; rep from * to last 2 sts, K2.

Row 2: K6; *P7, K4; rep from * to last 2 sts, K2.

Row 3: Rep Row 1.

Row 4: Rep Row 2.

Row 5: Rep Row 1.

Row 6: Rep Row 2.

Row 7: K2, P4; *C7B, P4; rep from * to last 2 sts, K2.

Row 8: Rep Row 2.

Row 9: K2, P4; *K2, K2tog, YO, K1, YO, sl 1, K1, PSSO, P4; rep from * to last 2 sts, K2.

Row 10: Rep Row 2.

Row 11: Rep Row 9.

Row 12: Rep Row 2.

Row 13: Rep Row 9.

Row 14: Rep Row 2.

Row 15: K2, P4; *C7B, P4; rep from * to last 2 sts, K2.

Row 16: Rep Row 2.

Repeat rows 1 through 16 for pattern.

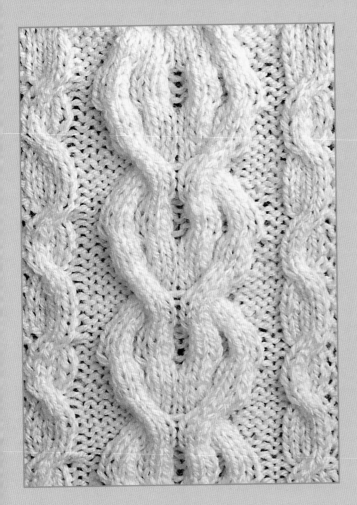

Rich Cable

Panel: 36 sts

STITCH GUIDE

C4F (Cable 4 Front): Slip next 2 sts to cable needle and hold at front, K2, then K2 from cable needle.

C4B (Cable 4 Back): Slip next 2 sts to cable needle and hold at back, K2, then K2 from cable needle.

C6F (Cable 6 Front): Slip next 3 sts to cable needle and hold at front, K3, then K3 from cable needle.

C6B (Cable 6 Back): Slip next 3 sts to cable needle and hold at back, K3, then K3 from cable needle.

T5F (Twist 5 Front): Slip next 3 sts to cable needle and hold at front, P2, then K3 from cable needle.

T5B (Twist 5 Back): Slip next 2 sts to cable needle and hold at back, K3, then P2 from cable needle.

INSTRUCTIONS

Row 1 (right side): P2, K4, P6, K12, P6, K4, P2.

Row 2: P6, K6, P12, K6, P6.

Row 3: P2, K4, P6, C6B, C6F, P6, K4, P2.

Row 4: P6, K6, P12, K6, P6.

Row 5: P2, C4F, P4, T5B, K6, T5F, P4, C4F, P2.

Row 6: P6, K4, P3, K2, P6, K2, P3, K4, P6.

Row 7: P2, K4, P4, K3, P2, K6, P2, K3, P4, K4, P2.

Row 8: P6, K4, P3, K2, P6, K2, P3, K4, P6.

Row 9: P2, K4, P2, (T5B) twice, (T5F) twice, P2, K4, P2.

Row 10: P6, K2, (P3, K2) twice, (K2, P3) twice, K2, P6.

Row 11: P2, C4B, (P2, K3) twice, P4, (K3, P2) twice, C4B, P2.

Row 12: P6, (K2, P3) twice, K4, (P3, K2) twice, P6.

Row 13: P2, K4, P2, (T5F) twice, (T5B) twice, P2, K4, P2.

Row 14: P6, K2, (K2, P3) twice, (P3, K2) twice, K2, P6.

Row 15: P2, K4, P4, T5F, K6, T5B, P4, K4, P2.

Row 16: P6, K6, P12, K6, P6.

Repeat Rows 3 through 16 for pattern.

Diamond Windows

Multiple: 11 + 13

STITCH GUIDE

M1 (Make one stitch): Make one st by picking up horizontal bar lying before next st and knitting into back of loop.

T3B (Twist 3 Back): Slip next st to cable needle and hold at back, K2, then P1 from cable needle.

T3F (Twist 3 Front): Slip next 2 sts to cable needle and hold at front, P1, then K2 from cable needle.

T5R (Twist 5 Right): Slip 3 sts to cable needle and hold at back, K2, then work P1, K2 from cable needle.

C4F (Cable 4 Front): Slip next 2 sts to cable needle and hold at front, K2, then K2 from cable needle.

C5B (Cable 5 Back): Slip next 3 sts to cable needle and hold at back, K2, then K3 from cable needle.

INSTRUCTIONS

Row 1 (right side): P6; *K1, P10; rep from * to last 7 sts, K1, P6.

Row 2: K6; *P1, K10; rep from * to last 7 sts, P1, K6.

Row 3: P5; *K3, P8; rep from * to last 8 sts, K3, P5.

Row 4: K5; *P3, K8; rep from * to last 8 sts, P3, K5.

Row 5: P4; *K5, P6; rep from * to last 9 sts, K5, P4.

Row 6: K4; *P5, K6; rep from * to last 9 sts, P5, K4.

Row 7: Rep Row 5.

Row 8: K2, M1, K2; *P5, (K2, M1) twice, K2; rep from * to last 9 sts, P5, K2, M1, K2.

Row 9: P5; *T5R, P8; rep from * to last 10 sts, T5R, P5.

Row 10: K5; *P2, K1, P2, K8; rep from * to last 10 sts, P2, K1, P2, K5.

Row 11: P4; *T3B, P1, T3F, P6; rep from * to last 11 sts, T3B, P1, TSF, P4.

Row 12: K4; *P2, K3, P2, K6; rep from * to last 11 sts, P2, K3, P2, K4.

Row 13: P3; *T3B, P3, T3F, P4; rep from * to last 12 sts, T3B, P3, T3F, P3.

Row 14: K3; *P2, K5, P2, K4; rep from * to last 12 sts, P2, K5, P2, K3.

Row 15: P2; *T3B, P1, P2tog, YO, P2, T3F, P2; rep from * to end of row.

Row 16: K2; *P2, K7, P2, K2; rep from * to end of row.

Row 17: P1; *T3B, P1, (P2tog, YO) twice, P2, T3F; rep from * to last st, P1.

Row 18: K1, P2; *K9, P4; rep from * to last 12 sts, K9, P2, K1.

Row 19: P1, K2; *P1, (P2tog, YO) 3 times, P2, C4F; rep from * to last 12 sts, P1, (P2tog, YO) 3 times, P2, K2, P1.

Row 20: Rep Row 18.

Row 21: P1; *T3F, P1, (P2tog, YO) twice, P2, T3B; rep from * to last st, P1.

Row 22: Rep Row 16.

Row 23: P2; *T3F, P1, P2tog, YO, P2, T3B, P2; rep from * to end of row.

Row 24: Rep Row 14.

Row 25: P3; *T3F, P3, T3B, P4; rep from * to last 12 sts, T3F, P3, T3B, P3.

Row 26: Rep Row 12.

Row 27: P4; *T3F, P1, T3B, P6; rep from * to last 11 sts, T3F, P1, T3B, P4.

Row 28: Rep Row 10.

Row 29: P5; *T5B, P8; rep from * to last 10 sts, T5B, P5.

Row 30: K2, K2tog, K1; *P5, K2, (K2tog, K1) twice; rep from * to last 10 sts, P5, K1, K2tog, K2.

Row 31: Rep Row 5.

Row 32: Rep Row 6.

Row 33: Rep Row 3

Row 34: Rep Row 4,

Row 35: Rep Row 1.

Row 36: Rep Row 2.

Repeat Rows 1 through 36 for pattern.

Hourglass Cable

Panel: 24 sts

STITCH GUIDE

Note: *This panel requires the use of two cable needles.*

T4B (Twist 4 Back): Slip next 2 sts to cable needle and hold at back, K2, then P2 from cable needle.

T4F (Twist 4 Front): Slip next 2 sts to cable needle and hold in front, P2, then K2 from cable needle.

SC (Special Cross): Slip 2 sts to cable needle and hold at front. Slip next 4 sts to 2nd cable needle and hold at back. K2, K4 from second cable needle, then K2 from first cable needle.

INSTRUCTIONS

Row 1 (right side): P6, T4F, K4, T4B, P6.

Row 2: K8, P8, K8.

Row 3: P8, K8, P8.

Row 4: K8, P8, K8.

Row 5: P8, SC, P8.

Row 6: K8, P8, K8.

Row 7: P6, T4B, K4, T4F, P6.

Row 8: K6, P2, K2, P4, K2, P2, K6.

Row 9: P4, T4B, P2, K4, P2, T4F, P4.

Row 10: K4, P2, K4, P4, K4, P2, K4.

Row 11: (P2, T4B) twice, (T4F, P2) twice.

Row 12: K2, (P2, K4) 3 times, P2, K2.

Row 13: (T4B, P2) twice, (P2, T4F) twice.

Row 14: P2, K4, P2, K8, P2, K4, P2.

Row 15: K2, P4, K2, P8, K2, P4, K2.

Row 16: P2, K4, P2, K8, P2, K4, P2.

Row 17: K2, P4, K2, P8, K2, P4, K2.

Row 18: P2, K4, P2, K8, P2, K4, P2.

Row 19: K2, P4, K2, P8, K2, P4, K2.

Row 20: P2, K4, P2, K8, P2, K4, P2.

Row 21: (T4F, P2) twice, (P2, T4B) twice.

Row 22: K2, (P2, K4) 3 times, P2, K2.

Row 23: (P2, T4F) twice, (T4B, P2) twice.

Row 24: K4, P2, K4, P4, K4, P2, K4.

Row 25: P4, T4F, P2, K4, P2, T4B, P4.

Row 26: K6, P2, K2, P4, K2, P2, K6.

Repeat Rows 1 through 26 for pattern.

Cable Crowns

Multiple: 15 + 5

STITCH GUIDE

CC1B (First Cable Crown Back): Slip next 3 sts to cable needle and hold at back; P1, K1, P1; then K3 from cable needle.

CC1F (First Cable Crown Front): Slip next 3 sts to cable needle and hold at front; K3, then K1, P1, K1 from cable needle.

CC2B (Second Cable Crown Back): Slip next 3 sts to cable needle and hold at back, K1, P1, K1, then K3 from cable needle.

CC2F (Second Cable Crown Front): Slip next 3 sts to cable needle and hold at front, K3, then P1, K1, P1 from cable needle,

INSTRUCTIONS

Row 1 (right side): K1, P3 *K3, (P1, K1) 3 times, K3, P3; rep from * to last st, K1.

Row 2: K4; *P3, (K1, P1) 3 times, P3, K3; rep from * to last st K1.

Row 3: K1, P3 *K3, (P1, K1) 3 times, K3, P3; rep from * to last st, K1

Row 4: K4; *P3, (K1, P1) 3 times, P3, K3; rep from * to last st K1.

Row 5: K1, P3; *CC1B, CC1F, P3; rep from * to last st, K1.

Row 6: K4; *K1, P1, K1, P7, K1, P1, K3; rep from * to last st, K1.

Row 7: K1, P3; *P1, K1, P1, K7, P1, K1, P3; rep from * to last st, K1.

Row 8: K4; *K1, P1, K1, P7, K1, P1, K3; rep from * to last st, K1.

Row 9: K1, P3; *P1, K1, P1, K7, P1, K1, P3; rep from * to last st, K1.

Row 10: K4; *K1, P1, K1, P7, K1, P1, K3; rep from * to last st, K1.

Row 11: K1, P3; *P1, K1, P1, K7, P1, K1, P3; rep from * to last st, K1.

Row 12: K4; *K1, P1, K1, P7, K1, P1, K3; rep from * to last st, K1.

Row 13: K1, P3; *P1, K1, P1, K7, P1, K1, P3; rep from * to last st, K1.

Row 14: K4; *K1, P1, K1, P7, K1, P1, K3; rep from * to last st, K1.

Row 15: K1, P3; *CC2F, CC2B, P3; rep from * to last st, K1.

Row 16: K4; *P3, (K1, P1) 3 times, P3, K3; rep from * to last st, K1.

Row 17: K1, P3; *K3, (P1, K1) 3 times, K3, P3; rep from * to last st, K1.

Row 18: K4; *P3, (K1, P1) 3 times, P3, K3; rep from * to last st, K1.

Row 19: K1, P3; *K3, (P1, K1) 3 times, K3, P3; rep from * to last st, K1.

Row 20: K4; *P3; (K1, P1) 3 times, P3, K3; rep from * to last st, K1.

Row 21: K1, P3; *K3, (P1, K1) 3 times, K3, P3; rep from * to last st, K1.

Row 22: K4; *P3, (K1, P1) 3 times, P3, K3; rep from * to last st, K1.

Row 23: K1, P3; *K3, (P1, K1) 3 times, K3, P3; rep from * to last st, K1.

Row 24: K4; *P3, (K1, P1) 3 times, P3, K3; rep from * to last st, K1.

Row 25: K1, P3; *K3, (P1, K1) 3 times, K3, P3; rep from * to last st, K1.

Row 26: K4; *P3, (K1, P1) 3 times, P3, K3; rep from * to last st, K1.

Row 27: K1, P3; *K3, (P1, K1) 3 times, K3, P3; rep from * to last st, K1.

Row 28: K4; *P3, (K1, P1) 3 times, P3, K3; rep from * to last st, K1.

Repeat Rows 5 through 28 for pattern.

69

Hearts

Panel: 34 sts

STITCH GUIDE

C4B (Cable 4 Back): Slip next 2 sts to cable needle and hold at back, K2, then K2 from cable needle.

T2B (Twist 2 back): Slip next st to cable needle and hold at back, K1, then P1 from cable needle.

T2F (Twist 2 Front): Slip next st to cable needle and hold at front, P1, then K1 from cable needle.

T3B (Twist 3 Back): Slip next st to cable needle and hold at back, K2, then P1 from cable needle.

T3F (Twist 3 Front): Slip next 2 sts to cable needle and hold at front, P1, then K2 from cable needle.

C2B (Cross 2 Back): Slip next st to cable needle and hold at back, K1, then K1 from cable needle.

C2F (Cross 2 Front): Slip next st to cable needle and hold at front, K1, then K1 from cable needle.

INSTRUCTIONS

Row 1 (right side): P1, (P6, K4, P6) twice, P1.

Row 2: K3, C2F, K2, P4, K2, C2B, K8, P4, K7 .

Row 3: P7, C4B, P7, T2B, T2F, P1, C4B, P1, T2B, T2F, P2.

Row 4: K2, P1, K2, P1, K1, P4, K1, P1, K2, P1, K7, P4, K7.

Row 5: P6, T3B, T3F, P6, K1, P1, T2B, T3B, T3F, T2F, P1, K1, P2.

Row 6: K2, (P1, K1) twice, P2, K2, P2, (K1, P1) twice, K6, P2, K2, P2, K6.

Row 7: P5, T3B, P2, T3F, P5, K1, T2B, T3B, P2, T3F, T2F, K1, P2.

Row 8: K2, P2, K1, P2, K4, P2, K1, P2, K5, P2, K4, P2, K5.